Jerome Beaty

J. Paul Hunter

Classroom Guide

THE NORTON INTRODUCTION TO LITERATURE

Shorter Fourth Edition

W · W · NORTON & COMPANY · NEW YORK · LONDON

Published simultaneously in Canada by Penguin Books
Canada Ltd, 2801 John Street, Markham, Ontario L3R
1B4

Printed in the United States of America

W. W. Norton & Company, Inc.
500 Fifth Avenue, New York, N. Y. 10110

W. W. Norton & Company, Ltd.
37 Great Russell Street, London WC1B 3NU

ISBN 0-393-95535-4

1 2 3 4 5 6 7 8 9 0

Contents

FICTION

P O E T R Y

Contents / iv

Contents / v

FICTION

TEACHING FICTION

The materials that follow offer informal, occasional, and nonprescriptive assistance to the teacher using the fiction section of The Norton Introduction to Literature. There is some commentary on most of the stories in the anthology, and for a good many there are questions that the instructor might want to use in class. Almost invariably some information reinforces or extends the guidance offered in the text itself, but this is not done systematically, nor is it the primary function of the Guide. Instead, I have aimed to share my thoughts on and experience in teaching the stories. Sometimes, then, the commentary will offer a reading or interpretation of the story, or alternative interpretations; when I have a firm opinion about the reading of a controversial story I will try to say so--not in order to close the issue but in order to avoid the false permissiveness that all of us fall into from time to time and that is the worst sort of intellectual bullying ("What am I holding in my hand?"). At other times I will try to suggest ways of opening or directing discussion that I have found work best for me for the particular story, and there will occasionally be warning of pitfalls that I have found in teaching the story or in teaching fiction in general. There will from time to time be questions and suggested topics for papers. There will often be comparisons and occasional suggestions for regrouping some of the stories into teaching units. I have not tried consciously to impose any fixed system of pedagogy, and I have tried to make the comments such that anyone teaching any selection of these stories in any order would find something in them that would be helpful (if only by arousing argument). Methods of teaching fiction are as various as the personalities and preferences of the teachers of fiction. I have tried to touch on various methods--aesthetic, historical, sociopolitical, among others--without consciously emphasizing any one unduly.

The first chapter, "Experiencing Fiction," is introductory, and, since it is designed to be discussed as it stands, I have not offered here alternative approaches. "Stories for Further Reading," on the other hand, belongs entirely to you, and I offer only minimal guidance.

And that's the story.

Edgar Allan Poe   The Cask of Amontillado   (p. 19)

I like to discuss a story like The Cask of
Amontillado early in the course because it is
familiar--many students will have read it in high
school and almost all will have heard of Edgar Allan
Poe; it is brief--instructor and students after a
couple of readings can hold the story in mind almost
in its entirety and virtually isolate details with a
mental pointer--and its structure and devices are
rather obvious (one might say that Poe lays it on
with a trowel, but of course one wouldn't). And it is
particularly useful in talking about plot because it
is a story about a plot as well as a story with a
plot. The macabre story is almost a fable for
readers, a paradigm of the relation between writer
and reader, with Montresor as author and Fortunato as
the unfortunate reader. So, you can tell your
students, if they don't want to get pinned to the
wall, they'd better pay attention.
      Montresor as author of the plot begins by
announcing that there is a plot--as authors
implicitly do by writing a story--and he announces
too that he considers a good plot one in which the
perpetrator-author doesn't get caught. This
challenges the reader to try to catch him, to try to
guess what will happen next. The author challenges
the reader's pride just as Montresor's dubious
amontillado challenges Fortunato's pride in his
knowledge of wine; the cask as wine and the cask of
amontillado as title are thus central to both plots.
(You might not want to call attention to the fact
that Fortunato is dressed as a fool.)
      The first thing a story must do, then, is to
arouse a certain amount of expectation or
anticipation, to get the reader to follow the author
or story--to read on--and to try to guess with the
story what is going to happen next or how it is going
to happen. In order for there to be suspense or
anticipation there must be some doubt or alternative
possibilities, and in order for there to be more than
one possibility, at least one possibility must turn
out to be wrong. False leads, then, are inherent in
plotting, and being aware of them (but not
necessarily aware that they are false) is essential
to participating in the story. Because I think such
alertness important, I like to ask students to stop
at certain points in reading a story and to write

down what they think might be going to happen next. Perhaps the first reasonable stopping place would be as Montresor and Fortunato are about to enter the vaults. A somewhat later one might be just after Fortunato's first coughing fit. You might even want to have the students stop reading as late as Montresor's stapling Fortunato to the wall, to see if they picked up the significance of the trowel (not too well buried in the mason joke).

If there are false leads, there must also be true leads, and you might want to suggest that even Montresor "plays fair" with Fortunato by ironic indications of his intentions, such as his agreeing that Fortunato will not die of a cough, his drinking to his victim's long life, his producing the trowel. These spots might make good stopping points too, or you might want to ask, once the story has been read, just when it becomes clear just what Montresor is up to.

I like to call attention at this point, or at least early in the discussion of plot, how much of the reader's guesswork is based on cause-effect, on some logic in the sequence of events and in the characters' motivations. We assume Montresor is leading Fortunato into the catacombs for a reason; in searching the story and our minds for the reason we notice the cough; when Montresor agrees that Fortunato will not die of a cough we either discard that possibility or believe the narrator to be a liar, or keep both possibilities in mind; if we notice the trowel and take it seriously, we have an answer. In one sense, plot and suspense seem to depend on logic--how could you guess what's to happen next in a wholly irrational universe? In what we can call the non-Western tradition, however, there is the suspense of expectation of sheer wonder, as in The Arabian Nights (The Thousand Nights and a Night) or tales of magic.

The plot structure seems fairly obvious here, with the exposition largely in (but not wholly confined to) the first three paragraphs; the rising action continuing until the climactic chaining of Fortunato to the wall (his recognition scene corresponding to that of many readers' recognition of precisely what Montresor has in mind); the action falling to the last paragraph's conclusion, and the leap of fifty years to the time of the narration (a gap we did not know existed, but which now might allow us to conjecture just why Montresor is narrating--or confessing).

There's more than enough matter even in this short and fairly simple story to fill an hour just talking about plot, but some instructors may want to assign the editorial matter in Chapters 3 and 4 right away and talk about focus and voice and character in relation to this story too.

There are only two characters here and Fortunato will be able to tell no tales, so only Montresor or an omniscient narrator can tell the story. It might be profitable to ask some or all of the students to try to rewrite this story in the third-person to see what's lost. You might point out to them that it is our tendency in reading fiction to take high moral ground and to damn all characters who are imperfect (for not being like ourselves). The first-person pulls us closer to the narrating characters, makes us cheer for him or her, as it were. When that narrator is a murderer as here (and in Graham Greene's Brighton Rock, or in Clockwork Orange where the punk isn't even very bright) or even just a snob, like Pip in Great Expectations, our emotions are more complicated. Is it that we understand or sympathize with the "sinner" more? Or is it that we say, "There but for the grace of God go I" and so think about our own fallibility (not yours, of course)? Or both?

This might be a good story to introduce the notion of character types or stereotypes. Why Italy? What period is the story set in? What do the students know or feel about the kinds of people and kinds of actions that took place then and there? You might want to bring up Machiavelli; or you might want to kill several birds with one stone by assigning a poem published just four years before this story was first published, Browning's My Last Duchess, and discuss more fully first-person murdering narrators, character types, literary tradition.

I vacillated in trying to decide what to follow this story with in the anthology. I stuck with The Most Dangerous Game both to reinforce the ideas of plot within and plot without a story and false leads and true, and in order to give instructor the option of skipping one or the other of the stories since either can be used to make most of the major points about plot. One of the interests of stories about plot, like Cask, is that in a sense it becomes a story about reading--the reader is doing the same thing as the person or persons not in on the plot, the author the same thing as the plotter. You might point out that detective stories, too, are stories about reading or interpreting. The reader tries to read back from effects to causes. The detective's work mirrors the recollective aspect of reading, the looking back to past details as we read on in a story, just as the plot of Montresor projects us forward in anticipation.

Many students will have read this story before,
perhaps in high school, and in my classes the vast
majority still like it a good deal. As a matter of
fact, it fairly consistently scores in the top three
or four when I ask students to rank the stories
they've read in order of preference. For many
instructors this will be a little surprising, and for
some more than a little disappointing. But it is a
"rattling good" adventure story with a good plot that
is well structured. I have to be very careful in
teaching this story not to be patronizing or offputting. This is not, after all, a poor story.

Assuming considerable student response, then,
you can plunge right in, to the structure or the
means by which the excitement of the story is
controlled and heightened. Students who have not read
the story before might be asked to stop reading at
the first break and write down their expectations
about how the story will develop and what in that
section gives rise to such expectations. It may be
well at this point to suggest that almost all plots
involve false expectations as well as "true" ones, or
foreshadowings, just as a good mystery story will
involve false clues leading to false suspicions. The
"true" expectations make the ending of the story
appear, when looked back upon, "inevitable," and the
false ones, cleverly used, make that inevitable
ending appear nonetheless "surprising." As I suggest
in the text, the best reader is not necessarily the
one who guesses the outcome correctly, but the one
who is most sensitive to all the possibilities, all
the expectation--a point that bears repetition.

There are two common, related, widely held, and
often unexpressed assumptions that might be
challenged in discussing this story. One is that
"mere adventure" stories or slick stories are devoid
of themes or thematic scope; the other is that "real
literature," as opposed to popular literature, is
cerebral or intellectual--literal detail in such
stories being only the embodiment of the abstract
"idea" of the story. Dangerous Game has a rather
clear theme that is announced in the first few
paragraphs; if its call for sympathy for the "huntee"
in a world divided between hunters and huntees is not
necessarily outright condemnation of hunting or
killing for any purpose, it is surely an appeal for
sympathy for the underdog and against violence,
urging the reader to put himself in the place of the
victim. That the story is set just after World War I
and the Russian Revolution, and that Zaroff and Ivan

are Cossacks (the most ferocious and loyal of the
adherents to the czar) does not seem wholly
accidental. The story thus has political and moral
thematic scope. Indeed the plot is almost too
contrived to illustrate that theme, too pat:
Rainsford, the hunter who believes in his total
difference from, and superiority to, the game he
hunts, is forced literally to put himself in the
position of the hunted. If this story falls short of
"literature," one might argue that it is not because
of its lack of "ideas," but because it is too
cerebral: the fiction or fable, the plot and
characters, being too dominated by theme, too
abstract and unlifelike.

The details of the hunt are clever, though it
would be interesting to try to argue which--Connell or
Hemingway--knew most about hunting, based solely on
internal evidence in the stories. The precise detail,
including details of character and characterization,
and the precise language in which the story is written
are not highly significant here. That's why the story
can be made into a good movie or TV play, or why it
can be retold in other words with relatively little
loss of power. This is not necessarily a flaw, of
course. It is, for one thing, testimony to the
strength of the story-line. And in this respect it is
typical of the yarn or tale, a story that can be
retold, can be transmitted orally with great variation
in words and sentence structures. It is, in fact, an
excellent illustration of history existing in large
measure independent of structure, and might be useful
in class for just that purpose.

Questions for Classroom Use

1. What expectations are aroused by the first
few sentences of dialogue in the story? How is each
of these expectations continued or reinforced,
fulfilled or disappointed? Once the nature of
Zaroff's "game" is clear, how is suspense maintained?
Do you ever really doubt the outcome? If you are
reasonably sure who is ultimately going to win the
"game," how do you explain the "excitement" or appeal
of such stories? Is "suspense" or "expectation" a
better word for describing your responses? How do you
know (by what means do you know) who is going to win
in this story? (How do you know who will win in a
John Wayne movie?) Can you tell with the same
certainty who is going to win an election? a football
game? an Olympics competition? Does your relative
certainty about the outcome of this story imply a
"view of reality" that you detect here? Can you
discover any specific evidence within the story of

that view? How much of your certainty of outcome derives from evidence within the story and how much from previous reading or film-watching experience?

2. Are there any details or actions in the story (such as Rainsford's falling overboard) that seem hard to believe? How do these affect your enjoyment of the story while you are reading it? your judgment of the story afterwards? Have you ever seen a film which you enjoyed until you thought about it later? until you saw it a second time? To what extent are "second thoughts" and second viewings or readings valid criteria for judging a work?

3. The first scene is presented almost entirely through dialogue. Are there any passages there that seem unnatural as conversation, as if they were clearly intended for the reader and not for the person spoken to? What is gained and what lost by this dramatic presentation?

4. In the first scene the discussion of hunting, the actual purpose of the trip, seems to be introduced casually into the conversation. Did it alert your expectations? In the light of later events, should it have? How is that discussion related to what happens later in the story? To what extent does the conversation define the specific theme of the story? How does Rainsford's dismissal of superstition and of "mental chill" as "pure imagination" relate to his theories of hunting?

5. Zaroff says that "instinct is no match for reason" and that "life is for the strong." How do these statements relate to Rainsford's earlier description of hunting? What are his reactions to Zaroff's statement? Is Zaroff's position logical? Are Rainsford's objections logical? Is there any significance in the fact that Zaroff's clothes fit Rainsford?

6. What does "game" in the title mean? To what extent is Zaroff's hunting a sport? Could he make the hunt more "interesting" by evening the odds, by giving the quarry more weapons or advantages? Does the fact that he does not do so throw any question on the validity of his arguments?

7. Zaroff is a Cossack and considers the overthrow of the czarist regime by the communists a debacle; he is a gentleman, a gourmet, a connoisseur. How do these details relate to his "game"? to his arguments? to the theme? Are there, then, political implications in the hunting-hunter theme of the story?

8. In a story that involves a considerable amount of action, the climactic action--the final fight between Zaroff and Rainsford--is not described. Can you think of any reasons for this omission? For

the paragraph leading up to the fight, the focus of
narration shifts for the first time from Rainsford;
why?

Ernest Hemingway   The Short Happy Life of Francis
     Macomber   (p. 39)

     With sex and violence, suspense and mystery,
clear prose and exotic setting, this story should be
surefire. It has a portable theme--to be a man one
must conquer fear of death--and patently follows the
initiation pattern that students will soon be used
to: after Macomber learns for the first time in his
life what it is to be without fear and knows he will
never be really afraid again, Wilson recognizes the
change: "he had seen men come of age before and it
always moved him. It was not a matter of their
twenty-first birthday. . . . More of a change than
any loss of virginity. . . . Made him into a man.
Women knew it too. No bloody fear."
     It may be well to get this theme out into the
open first, perhaps by asking about the title: Don't
we usually think of happy lives being long? How short
was Macomber's? One answer that ought to come out is
that it lasted only from the moment he felt free of
fear to the moment he was shot. From this point it's
usually easy to work in the conception of the story
as initiation, a rite of passage or coming of age, if
you want to teach this as such a story.
     I usually leap from one end of the story to the
other, from the title to the death of Macomber. Is it
ironic that just when he became a man and could
really live, he has to die? Why couldn't he have
lived on, patched things up with his wife, and lived
a good, long life? What would have happened if
Macomber had not died? These questions might make
interesting paper assignments that would reveal a
good deal about how much the writer of the paper
understood about the Hemingway story. Of course
Macomber does not just die--he's killed. He's shot by
his wife. Deliberately or accidentally? Consciously
or unconsciously? In exploring this incident we open
up most if not all the important aspects of the
story, and discussing it will serve to show how we
amass and use evidence from the text, how we infer
from facts, and how we construct patterns from the
facts and inferences. The class will have to try to
describe the character of Macomber and Margot, their
"set" and living conditions, the nature of their
marriage, and their life patterns (or style) in
general. In doing so, the information will have to be
evaluated in terms of where it's coming from--from

action, dialogue, one character's thoughts, another's. You might want to raise the question, while the class is discussing focus of narration (Chapter 3), why it is that though the focus shifts often throughout the story--we even get into the lion's mind--we are not allowed inside Margot's mind when she is aiming and firing the fatal shot. Would it help if we could know what was going on inside her mind?

Discussing the story either in terms of the initiation theme or in terms of the killing of Macomber will inevitably lead to its time structure. Some will no doubt want to begin their discussion there--and, indeed, the story is placed in the anthology as an example of suspense of plot expectation. Some will want to discuss its structure purely in terms of the story itself, while others-- and this too is intended in the arrangement--will want to compare its structure with that of Dangerous Game. As the story now stands--that is, as Hemingway structured it--the hunting theme and the marital theme are introduced immediately, in the first scene. If the story had begun at the chronological beginning, with the first lion hunt and Macomber's act of cowardice, the hunting-fear theme would predominate; though the relationship of Macomber and his wife could have been introduced immediately thereafter, it still would be not only second but perhaps secondary, an offshoot of the hunting theme. Now when we ask "What will happen next?" we usually mean both in the hunting and in the marriage. Game serves as a useful contrast in that it is chronological and focused solely on hunting.

Like Game, Macomber deals with dangerous or adventurous hunting where the life of the hunter is often at stake, but unlike Game it endorses the hunter's mystique that involves all kinds of moral and "masculine" values. Macomber, I fear, reeks of macho values, or machismo. It may not be antiwoman, but it does seem patently hostile to American women at least (Wilson has found them to be domineering and cruel). Nor can it be claimed that Hemingway is merely giving insight into the way other men's macho minds work: Margot behaves according to the code-- when Macomber shows cowardice she openly kisses Wilson, and the brave hunter is visited in his bed by the wife of the cowardly unmale. And remember Wilson's description of the loss of fear as greater than any loss of mere virginity.

What is the effect of this theme or view or set of values in the story on our appreciation or evaluation of it, and how can we cope with it in class? Do women students--or instructors--object to

these stories? laugh at them? find them boring? or
childish? Are these attitudes as represented in the
stories, to male students and instructors, still
prevalent, or do they seem at least historically
accurate, no matter whether laudable or laughable?
Can women and men learn from these stories? That is,
is the view of reality as seen through the eyes of
traditional sexism with its typecasting of roles and
values so well presented that, whatever our own
attitudes, we can say, "Yes, if one held these
values, this is how the world would look"? Can we--
must we--condemn a work that operates out of a value
system wholly different from our own? Can we argue,
on the other hand, that we must understand such
visions of reality before true communication and
change can occur?

Ambrose Bierce   An Occurrence at Owl Creek Bridge (p.
    66)

    As I suggested in the text, this story scarcely
could exist were it not for the focus shifting in
section three to Peyton Farquhar's consciousness for
much of the rest of the story. Indeed, between the
sergeant's stepping aside at the end of the first
section and the final paragraph nothing much
happens--Farquhar merely hangs.
    You might want to ask the students about the
second section and what would happen to their
expectations if it were removed. This is not exactly
a false lead, but like a false lead it distracts the
reader from anticipating correctly or certainly. Of
course it does something else: by characterizing
Farquhar as patriotic, dedicated, and daring, and by
revealing that his crime was an entrapment, the
reader's sympathies are entirely enlisted on his
side. You might ask how many students basically side
with the Union and whether any of them wanted
Farquhar to be "caught." If not, you may ask, why
not? Getting us on Farquhar's side, to cheer him on
and to hope for his escape is, of course, an
important element in the strategy of the story.
    There are a number of clues in the story
pointing to what is actually happening. You might ask
the students to identify them. You might also ask
them in advance to keep a brief record of their
expectations as they read through the story.
    You may want to call attention to some of the
minute, realistic details in section one, and have
the students identify others, and ask them why there
are so many and what they do. One of the functions
seems to be to slow down, almost stop the fictional
clock--there's so much description that we seem to be
looking at a tableau or still picture. This tends
subtly to identify the narrative authority of the
story with Farquhar, who, in the fourth paragraph,
notes how slowly the driftwood moves, and allows us
to accept later his illusions of how much time is
passing and what events are occurring.
    The scrupulously realistic detail may have
another function. There is a fairly common feeling
among many of us and many of our students that this
is essentially a story with a gimmick and, therefore,
not "serious" fiction (a notion reinforced, perhaps,

by the fact that it is a story often taught in high school, where, as we know, serious fiction is not seriously considered). Though it may seem contrived to us, it is very likely that when first published, like Jane Eyre a couple of generations earlier or the stories of Guy de Maupassant about this time, this story was considered "realistic." For adventure stories and romances, the popular fiction of the time, usually ended happily, and heroes did miraculously escape. That Farquhar did not, that he was misled by the fiction his mind made up, may, in context, appear bitterly realistic. The story, then, may ask us to contrast wishes, wish-fulfilling fantasies--including the kind of heroism suggested in section two--with the cold external realities. Just as Poe makes us for a time identify with a villain, here we emotionally identify with a hero who doesn't make it.

Could this be the time when you'll want to ask the students about their response to stories with happy and those with unhappy endings when you want to address the frequent student complaint that all the stuff they read in English courses is "pessimistic"?

William Faulkner   A Rose for Emily (p. 73)

The most striking and memorable thing about A Rose for Emily is its shocking revelation at the end, and that, naturally, is what most students--even those who have read the story before, perhaps in high school--will want to talk about. You might want to talk about focus and voice, but it is probably advisable to give students their head. For one thing, it is rather easy to turn such a discussion to the recuperative aspect of reading--that is, how later things in a story make us selectively recall and reconsider earlier ones. By way of comparison, I like to point out how the typical structure of detective stories--a kind most students are familiar with--forces you by the revelation at the end to go back over the story recalling "clues." In Emily, of course, you don't know that you are working toward a revelation--or do you? Is there a kind of expectation based on the very lack of an obvious "plot," an obvious sense of suspense or curiosity? Does the fact that you are reading a story mean that you have to expect something--or otherwise it would not be a story?

When you are talking about later events in the story recalling earlier ones you are in this story obviously talking about sequence, not necessarily chronology, for one of the more obvious characteristics of this story is its elaborate and complex treatment of historical time. (This manipulation of the history of Emily, you may want to point out, is a dramatic example of structure.) It may be useful to have the students write a paper or draw up a chart for class discussion of the time scheme in the story. It highlights the structuring, reveals how many time signals and specific dates there are in the story, ensures careful reading, and results in enough differences (I know every time I try to work it out I get a few more specific dates and a few different answers) to ensure a lively class discussion.

Why so unorthodox a time scheme? (If one of your students does not, with more or less exasperation, bring this up, you just may have to do so yourself.) I always have at least one student who believes authors are deliberately, even perversely, obscure, and another who thinks "obscurity" is a sign of "art" or "modernity" or both. I'm afraid I usually put such students off and say, "Well, let's talk about this story for a while, and I'll come back to that question." If I don't do that I find myself forced into giving my "reading" of the story to "justify" its structure. It is possible, however, to deal with the issue of plot manipulation which often arises at this point. Isn't the purpose of the complicated time scheme to delay the revelation or to put the reader off the scent? Probably so. How does that differ, then, from Connell's shifting focus from Rainsford to Zaroff when Rainsford jumps off the cliff? Wasn't that, too, just to increase the suspense? Why is some manipulation bad and another not? If you have not mentioned Hemingway's refusal to enter Margot Macomber's mind at the crucial moment, this might be the time to do it, or, if you have, you may wish to recall what you have no doubt pointed out: that even if we were to know what Margot was thinking we might not know her real motive, for she probably did not consciously know herself, and this is a significant part of the story. So we cannot know whether manipulation is good or bad unless we explore what the relationship is between the structure and the meaning of the story.

If some students attack the story hard enough, others are sure to leap to its defense, and one defense that is fairly obvious is more than likely to come up: the time shifts are mimetic; this is the way people tell stories, and this is the way memory and gossip and oral narrative in general work. Now you're forced to be the devil's advocate. That reasoning may explain shifting time in general but it does not help these shifts, these particularities, in particular.

If the world, or the world of the classroom, were an orderly place, you would always reach exactly this point and turn to the second paragraph of the story. I want to talk about structure and time scheme and all that I've mentioned, but I also really want to get to that second paragraph, so I get there one way or the other, even if it means saying, at some irrelevant point, "Speaking of the second paragraph. . . . " What is there in this paragraph that suggests that the narrator, the voice, is not just spinning a yarn, happening to tell the story in this seemingly casual way? It usually does not take too long for someone to point out that the description of Emily's house "lifting its stubborn and coquettish decay" is not entirely innocent or accidental, that the noun and both adjectives relate to more than just Emily's house. And, if the class has brought up the time element, it should not be too long before someone mentions that there are the three specific times suggested in the paragraph--the 1870s, when the house was built; the more-or-less present with garages and gasoline pumps, probably the 1920s; and the 1860s, the time of the battle of Jefferson in the Civil War. Emily is joining the Civil War dead in the cemetery. It is at this point that I like to look forward to the next paragraph--"Miss Emily had been a tradition, a duty, and a care"--and back to the first--"the men [went to her funeral] through a sort of respectful affection for a fallen monument"--and ask what the title means.

Can this story really be a tribute to someone whose gray hair is on the pillow next to a skeleton? What are we supposed to think of Miss Emily Grierson? Now, perhaps, is the time to recall not only the focus of the story but the voice. Who is speaking? What is he like? To what extent are we supposed to share his values?

The answer to the first question is easy--he's a (self-appointed) white male representative of the townspeople. The answer to the second question is just a bit more complicated. If you have discussed the sexism in Macomber, there should be no difficulty in identifying the sexism here: the men go to the funeral out of affection and respect, the women out of curiosity, wanting a peek inside the house; only a woman would believe Colonel Sartoris's gallant lie; the very title suggests a male tribute to a "lady." Sexism in A Rose for Emily should generate good papers or a good discussion; nor is this a suggestion for a merely fashionable subject for the 1980s, for the question of the narrator's attitude toward Emily and ours toward the narrator is central in our reading of the story.

The question does not involve only gender roles, of course, but the values of the whole town or society (and the attitude of the story toward the attitude of the town). How are we supposed to feel about Colonel Sartoris? He gallantly remits Emily's taxes and protects her pride by telling her that the town owed Emily's father money. Yet it was Colonel Sartoris's edict that decreed that Negro women should not appear on the streets without an apron. How are we supposed to feel about Emily's proud refusal both to lie and to obey the law when she purchases arsenic? Matters of sex and race and class permeate the story, bringing a whole bygone society back to life. Good or bad, it's gone, and not even Emily can pretend that it is not dead. Does this suggest a reason for the manipulation of time sequence, a spatializing of the fifty or sixty years following the Civil War? And who is Emily? What is she a monument to, and why does she deserve a rose?

You might want to ask--perhaps as a paper assignment--whether the story affirms the values of that society, describes them objectively and noncommittally, treats them ironically, critically, nostalgically? Do we need to distinguish between "the story" (that is, Faulkner, or even the reader) and the voice? Is the story obliged to evaluate the narrator's values and those of the society he represents?

Can your students imagine this story told any other way, perhaps as The Telltale Heart, beginning, "The dozens of insults of Homer Barron I had borne as best I could, but when he ventured to injure my good name before all the town I vowed revenge"?

Mordecai Richler   The Summer My Grandmother Was
      Supposed to Die (p. 79)

This is the first story in the anthology to deal with an experience that many students will think of as close to or potentially close to their own, dealt with in a way that they think they might be able to emulate. Though the elements of revenge, cruelty, courage, and imagination may be extracted from the first stories and related to the student's own life, The Summer My Grandmother Was Supposed to Die seems to cry out for a personal narrative from the student.

I don't like to teach this kind of story first in a course because it gets us--and I really mean to include msyelf--using stories to talk only about ourselves, reducing them to our terms instead of going out to meet them on their own and thereby broadening our own perspectives. But I do want to treat personal narrative fairly early to make sure that our reading and discussion are not merely cerebral exercises or academic games.

So after I have talked about literature for a week or so in a more or less "objective" way and had the class write at least one paper critically treating a more or less technical aspect of narrative structure, I like to ask the students to read a personal narrative like Richler's and to write one of their own, suggesting that it might be well to choose a real episode to write about. And I ask them to be very conscious of the questions they are asking, the choices they are making, the problems they face. How do you select an experience to write about? What makes it seem like good material for a story? Where do you begin? How do you get your reader's attention? How do you decide what to put in and what to leave out, what to tell when? How do you tell a story?

You might apply some of these questions to the Richler story. The opening of that story may seem easy to explain, natural: he begins with the doctor's decree that the boy's grandmother has less than a month to live. Though she lives for more than four months more, the story seems bounded by diagnosis and death. But very soon the story shifts back seven years to the death of the grandfather, the grandmother's stroke soon thereafter, and her coming to live with the narrator's family. The seven years prior to the gangrene are divided by the mother's illness, the temporary removal of the grandmother to the home, and her return--precipitated by the narrator's blunder. It is not until near the end of the story that we learn the full force of the title and that the structure of the story is justified-- from "supposed to die" in the doctor's terms back to the story of the grandfather, his first marriage, second marriage, and death, and forward to the death of the grandmother and the new gloss on the phrase "supposed to die." If the title does not tease us into attention, the third brief paragraph should: isn't it unnatural, monstrous, for Muttel's mother to want her own mother to die?

Some discussion might be generated by asking students at first to point out the realistic detail in the story (the Jewish milieu, the streets of Montreal, the apparently digressive details of the thoughts and activities of small boys--from peeping to scatology, to popular culture, sibling rivalry, baseball) and how that contributes to a sense of actuality. But, you might ask the students, isn't its apparent actuality undermined by artful structuring, the rearrangement of the chronology and such "literary" devices as the verbal play in the title that defines the structure?

How about the students' own narratives? Have any of them rearranged the time sequence of the history? Are the details selected or arranged to "make a point" or embody a theme? Does "telling a story" mean distorting reality?

The story would not be the same if its narrator could have told it moment by moment or at least episode by episode as it happened (though of course he was only seven when his grandfather died and younger than our students when his grandmother finally died). Doesn't memory inevitably distort? When we know how things turn out, we can go back and select those things that were important in making it turn out that way (like film clips from a game). That, we must agree, is distortion. Surely, then, things written down immediately--like Pamela's letters (so we can't say "in the heat of the moment," can we?)--are truer: they tell things more as they really are. Perhaps one of the students wrote a narrative that he or she remembered but that was also recorded at the time in a journal or diary. Isn't the immediate, personal account the more accurate? Knowing others won't read it we tell our diary the truth--don't we? You might ask if any students are embarrassed by their old diaries, if they can see their self-deception, or "acting." Isn't the writer of the diary really a persona or two personae we construct for the purposes of writing and reading the diary, you may ask. Isn't the self projected in the diary a fiction of sorts, someone we would like to be, or someone like fictional characters we admire? Isn't the writer an "interested party"? There may be ways, then, in which disinterested or inquisitive memory may be more rather than less accurate than the immediate transcription.

A good deal of this has to do with focus and voice. The voice in a remembered story is the older narrator, the focus the younger acting character. Even in a diary focus and voice may be to some degree different, depending on how much we make ourselves the hero of our own lives.

The purpose of raising to consciousness the way narration distorts experience is not to belittle narration, but, on the contrary, to attempt to suggest to the students that learning to read stories, learning how people tell stories, and what's involved, can make them aware of how they make stories out of their own experiences, and how they try, through narrative, to make sense of their own lives.

4 CHARACTERIZATION

Toni Cade Bambara   My Man Bovanne (p. 95)

This might be a good story for one of my favorite assignments: "Rewrite this story or a portion of this story using a different focus and voice." How would Hazel be presented by an omniscient narrator? by one of her children? How would Joe Lee's and Elo's portrait of their mother differ? What would Bovanne think was going on? You might want to select a very brief section of the story and ask the students to rewrite it from several different points of view.

Bovanne may not seem to many students to be a story like The Cask of Amontillado in which first-person narration makes the narrator more sympathetic. In a politically oriented class, however, someone is sure to come down hard on Hazel for her lack of militancy, perhaps even lack of racial pride (and, perhaps by assuming Hazel represents fully the author's political and other views, on Bambara herself). In the second paragraph, for example, there's the suggestion that "Black Power" messes young people up "till they can't be civil to old folks," and there are many other passages in which Hazel seems to dismiss or denigrate the political ideas and actions of the young blacks. (We know Bambara is a dedicated activist, by the way, but that should not be brought in from outside the story until the implications of the details of the story itself are exhausted.) You might want your students to define just what Hazel's political position is by amassing evidence from the story. Do her children understand her position?

A student attack on Hazel or on what one thinks the story is saying might bring up the whole question of how we measure the "reliability" of dramatic utterances, how much the story stands behind remarks made by the characters, including the narrator. How do the students evaluate Elo's statement that there is no generation gap in the black community? How do we infer Hazel's view? How do we infer where the story stands with regard to Elo's and Hazel's views? How do we go about "proving" our case? How old is Hazel? Her son Joe Lee says sixty-one (or more?); Hazel denies it. Who's right? With luck, this might get a pretty good discussion going, and if it doesn't degenerate into assertions of mere opinion or of

will, the students may teach themselves how to dig
into a story for evidence.

Hazel's age, sex, ethnic identity, and political and
other opinions may occasion the question of how we relate
to characters significantly different from ourselves (some
students will be black, female, activist, but few over
sixty). Don't young people tend to identify with the young
characters? Do your students take the side of Elo or Joe
Lee against their mother? My experience has been that more
often than I anticipated they do not, and that it's not
until I say something like, "Well, now, how would you feel
if Hazel were your mother and behaving this way?" that
perspectives begin to change to what we would expect to be
the norm. It's not that I want them to condemn Hazel,
certainly, but I do want them to see how their reading of
stories has taken them out of themselves, away from what
we often assume are ego-bound identifications and self-
interest, an effect I consider both proper and good. If it
has not done so, then I have to work the other way. Here,
for example, I have to rub them up against the passage in
which Elo   puts her hand on her mother only lightly and
tentatively and Hazel is hurt by her daughter's not having
confidence in her mother's acceptance and love. I have
also found what at first seems strange and then all too
understandable an attitude among students toward sex and
the un-young. How do your students regard Hazel's
unconventional morality, her "Mama comfort," her intention
to give Bovanne a good bath and rubdown? How do they
regard her earthy language? This might be a good point in
the course at which to talk about the function of language
in characterization as well as in other aspects of short
stories.

So I circle right back: ask the students to put this
story in the words of an omniscient narrator, or to
summarize it in their own words. I'll bet it loses
something in the translation. Some stories, like The Most
Dangerous Game, don't. You may not want to make this seem
a value judgment, but you might ask from time to time
which stories seerm to be re-tellable in different words
and which seem bound to their own.

Henry James   The Real Thing (p. 99)

If The Cask of Amontillado is a story about plot or
plotting, The Real Thing is a story about character and
characterization, and that, plus its quality, is why it is
here. The chapter suggests how I read the story--real
ladies and gentlemen are useless as models for or
representation of ladies and gentlemen precisely because
they are real, and reality is made up of stereotypes.
Major and Mrs. Monarch are only useful as models for
stereotyped stories. You might want to point out that this

paradox is prepared for in the first paragraph by the
"paradoxical law" that people who looked famous were ne<
famous and vice versa. Both these paradoxes are debatab
and sooner or later--but perhaps later, toward the end
your discussion of the story--you may want to raise the
issue of the truth of the story, whether it is the real
thing, but by that time you may also have laid the
groundwork for discussing the reliability of the narrat

And something you may have to clear up first is
the whole conception of class. I find that my
students have great trouble with this concept,
particularly as it appears in James or Trollope or
any late nineteenth- or early twentieth-century
English work (the American-born James being in many
ways more English than the English). Many know
better, but they insist on using "rich" and "upper
class" as synonyms. They have to be reminded about
"the vulgar rich" and the "impoverished genteel" and
many informed for the first time that anyone who
works for a living, no matter how rich--or mannerly--
is, at best, <u>middle</u> class. It is possible that
without some discussion of class the full poignancy
of the story (as, in the final paragraph, "it was
dreadful to see them emptying my slops") will not
fully come across. Not that this poignancy will go
unchallenged--"Why shouldn't they empty slops?
Somebody's got to do it. Why are they any better than
anyone else? If they have to make a buck and they
have no other skills, then they just have to do the
best they can." Can an egalitarian read with sympathy
this apparently elitist story? (We are back to
whether a 1980s feminist or civil libertarian can
read <u>A Rose for Emily</u> with sympathy.) How one deals
with different, especially unacceptable, political,
social, and moral values in reading and appreciating
literature is an issue that must be confronted in any
course treating literature, especially that of other
times or cultures. I want my students to take values
and literature seriously, as I am sure most of you do
too, so too latitudinarian a position may subvert our
purposes. On the other hand, I do not want to
reinforce what I find is an already entrenched bias
against appreciating or applauding anything that
fails to confirm our own vision and views, for this
clearly works against the understanding and sympathy
it seems to me that the study of the humanities and
especially the study of literature are meant to
encourage. I cannot imagine myself tolerating any
modern European or American story affirming torture,
human sacrifice, or cannibalism, for example. But I
think I might be able to accept an Aztec or African
tale which does so (though I am not really sure). You
may disagree even with this hesitant position; you

may draw the line elsewhere. This is a very shadowy area, but the issues are real and important, and, if we are not to sterilize our discipline, I believe we must get it out in the open, in front of the class, with all our prejudices and uncertainties hanging out. What do you think?

When I feel I've sufficiently discussed character and characterization, stereotypes and class distinctions, art and reality, and perhaps literature and values, and life, I like to turn to the very end of the story: "my friend Hawley repeats that Major and Mrs. Monarch did me a permanent harm, got me into false ways. If it be true I'm content to have paid the price--for the memory." That the story is a "memory" of the somewhat distant past is suggested in the very first sentence of the story--"in those days." I am not sure what the value of the memory is that has made it worth so much to the narrator. The memory surely is not pleasant--he hated seeing them empty slops, he had to turn them away after about a week, he does not know whether he did them any good, what their fates were. He does not seem to mean that the memory was in the "lesson"--that art is the illusion of reality and not the representation of it--for the price he has paid apparently is a lessening of his artistic ability ("permanent harm," "false ways"). I'd like to think that James, being James, is turning the screw of the paradox once again, so that if the real thing is not a good model for art, then perhaps what is good for art is not good for our real lives, our humanity. That experience which weakened his art made him a better human being (or "real person"). As I say elsewhere in the text, I do not mind parading my uncertainties before the class when they are real and earned--that is, when I have at least worked at resolving them.

Part of the "earning" here may be trying to come to terms with the character of the narrator himself. He is not a successful enough artist not to want paying "sitters" and commercial work doing book illustrations, yet he is quick enough to point out that his professional judgment is not that of a barber or tailor (that he is not merely commercial, a tradesman). His mind is subtle enough to see things paradoxically, shrewd enough to recognize that since Claude Rivet only painted landscapes he would sacrifice nothing in recommending the Monarchs to him for their portraits, and decorous enough not to say so. After you have done so to your own satisfaction, you might want your students to go through the story as carefully and thoroughly as possible, finding as many details as possible that characterize the narrator. They can then report their results in a paper or discuss them in class. One question that you may want to raise yourself is what, precisely, is the narrator's attitude toward the country-house class? or toward the Monarchs, for that matter. His distress at seeing them down on their luck and emptying slops to the contrary notwithstanding (or is distress his full feeling?), isn't there a kind of contempt, even hostility in his attitude? Perhaps a kinder way of getting at this is to ask the students to try to deduce from the story exactly what the narrator believes is the value of art and the role of the artist in society.

Doris Lessing   Our Friend Judith (p. 118)

     This is one of those stories about which some students are likely to say, "Nothing happens," so it might be a good idea from the beginning to ask them to list all the things that do happen in the story. In a sense the students are right--many of the things that happen do not happen in the story but are told about by the narrator or Betty or Judith herself. It's probably important for them both to know that a good deal happens and to understand why it doesn't seem that anything happens. It might be useful, then, to have them show how the interesting things in the story--Judith's affair with Luigi, the young cat's labor and delivery--are distanced by having to be reported. This is an aspect of focus--a kind of mediated mediation--not directly treated in Chapter 3 that might be useful to discuss at this point: its effect, its relation to the play-within-the-play or "embedded" narration, perhaps its relation to dialogue. There is little sense of suspense; the major question we ask while reading the story is not "What's going to happen next?". And that's probably what the students mean by "Nothing happens."
     If it is going to take so much of the anticipation away, why, then, have the friend narrate and why have so many things told to her? What's gained? To what questions, what other centers of interest is the reader's attention shifted?
     Of course if you ask the questions that way and if you are following the chapters in the text, the brighter students will put two and two together and come up with Judith's character as the center of interest, following with the question, "What's Judith like?" Good enough, but you will have to look out for--or hope for?--the reductive readings: she's this cool-seeming, intellectual, respectable type who's really all fire and like that underneath; she lives one kind of life in the open and another in secret.

With any luck, you'll get a more contemporary and subtle but perhaps equally reductive reading--Judith is her own woman, who does not need a man to lean on or depend on, but lives in the world, has her profession, and does her own thing in a liberated way that used to be thought of as only the province and right of men. If both those readings come up--or if you can provoke the other once one comes up--your problem will not be to arouse discussion but to keep things in hand.

Both to control irresponsible or partisan debate or to substitute for that argument should it not come up, it may be useful at one point or another to suggest that this is a detective story, but that what the detection seeks is not the solution of a crime but the understanding of a character. You might want to start with the narrator's rejection of the two smug assumptions in the first two paragraphs--that Judith is a typical English spinster and that she has given up. The narrator's experience of other spinsters, her aunts, suggests first that Judith does resemble them but that they are not fossilized, conventional old maids; and suggests then that the narrator may have to change her "pitying" attitude toward women without men. The narrator then sadly confesses that through her own stupidity she lost her chance to find out what Judith and her life are really like. We need to get on the table what the lost opportunity was and whether the narrator really blundered. But suppose we can read through the story, beyond the stupid blunder in a way the narrator cannot? Imagine a detective story in which Holmes or Ellery Queen is stumped but the reader is left with what seems to be a sufficient number of clues to solve the crime.

This story, as the narrator suggests, should modify our notions of the typical English spinsters, largely through our knowledge of Judith. How is our stereotype modified? Is it wholly reversed? Drastically changed? Changed in all superficial aspects (celibacy, prudery) but retaining some of its inner nature?

The narrator sets forth some clues baldly in the three revelatory incidents: the dress that Judith refuses to wear (Judith says, "One surely ought to stay in character, wouldn't you say?"); the refusal to castrate the tomcat: ("It's the nature of a male cat to rampage lustfully about, and therefore it would be morally wrong for Juidith to have the cat fixed"); Judith's ultimate "apology" to the young man who damaged her flat (". . . having chosen that you should have it, it was clearly an unwarrantable infringement of your liberty to make any conditions

at all.") "The facts about Judith, then, are all in
the open," the narrator says, "unconcealed, and plain
to anyone who cares to study them; or, as it became
clear she feels, to anyone with the intelligence to
interpret them." The challenge is thrown in the
reader's face: Are we intelligent enough to interpret
the facts with any certainty? (I'm not sure I am, by
the way.) Perhaps students should be asked to stop
reading the story at this point, as they had been
asked to stop reading suspenseful stories at certain
points, and here asked to use their intelligence to
"interpret" Judith's character as they were earlier
asked to predict plot developments. Then they might
compare their conclusions here with what they think
of Judith at the end of the story. Regardless of how
successful the predictions are, this should show
students that as readers they collect, recollect, and
project as they read in areas other than plot.

    What sort of image do the students have of the
narrator? She calls herself stupid yet sees and
interprets much evidence convincingly (the two rows
of books from Judith's former lovers, for example),
but at the same time she seems to fall into such
banalitites as saying oh, yes, Judith would have a
cat and she must be lonely sometimes. Is the narrator
"interfering" when she asks Judith about her leaving
Italy? Do we agree with Judith that the narrator is
"stupid" for using the word "interfere"? What do the
students make of Judith's failure to understand why
the narrator, Betty, and the Rinieri's "care"? And
who is right about why the cats gather to watch the
painful labor of Judith's pregnant kitten? What do
your students make of Judith's reaction to Luigi's
killing the kitten? Why, you might ask, are the other
women friends involved in the story at all; why is it
our rather than my friend Judith? Why is Betty
involved? (How much do we learn about her?)

    I'm putting lots of this in the form of
questions not as a pedagogical device, though I do
think these and similar questions ought to stimulate
lots of discussion, but because I feel they are real
questions, that is, those without single, simple
answers. Or, to put it another way, I'm not sure I
understand exactly what we are to make of Judith, or
whether what we are to make of the story is the
difficulty of making anything about people's
characters. One of the reasons I like Lessing so much
is that she, like Lawrence, gets the reader to make
human judgments about human actions and character,
and that there is no one "literary" answer planted
symbolically or structurally in the story. This is
not to say that Lessing and Lawrence have not made
judgments, but that the judgments are complex,

variable, individual; your judgments of the human
issues in the story define your character, not your
moral or intellectual worth necessarily, but what you
are "like." Since our egos make us to some extent
want to "like" the creator of the fiction we are
reading, we try to understand and intuit that vision.
In inviting us into their worlds such writers "teach"
us, not judgments or maxims, but how to judge.

Students are often uneasy with this kind of
openness--not just a paradox or literary irony or
structural ambivalence but an openness that tests the
readers' characters rather than their intelligence
alone. They're especially uneasy when you can't or
won't give them some answers to write in their
notebooks. So it might be best in some classes to
hold off on this story until you're well into the
course. On the other hand, if you have a sharp,
articulate, aggressive group, it would be well to
throw this at them early--and not let them off the
hook with modish, ready-made answers.

5 SYMBOLS

Nathaniel Hawthorne   <u>Young</u> <u>Goodman</u> <u>Brown</u> (p. 135)

This deceptively simple story works well in
class, I find, and is particularly useful fairly early
in an introductory course. There may be a few students
who will see none of the allegorical implications and
little if any of even the more conventional aspects of
the initiation theme. Most, however, will see some of
the "clues," and classes often come to life as they
pile on detail after detail; even those students who
saw nothing at first will get into the act before the
discussion is turned to the less obvious elements in
the story. There will be an initial sense of
accomplishment and contribution, then a deep breath,
further discussion, and, one hopes, greater
illumination.

The initial stage of the class discussion, if
you are lucky, may wind up with something like this:
The innocent hero learns that there is evil even in
the best of us, that all men are sinners, that we all
partake of original sin. This participation in sin is
represented in the story by the townspeople's
participating at night and in the woods in a satanic
version of their daytime religious services and
rituals. Salem, the scene of the notorious witch
trials, is thus an appropriate setting. Though
"goodman" is a title merely meaning "husband," the
allegorical weight of "good man" is clearly
appropriate; "young" clearly suggests "innocent";
"Brown" is so common a name that, like Tom Jones,
perhaps, it can suggest "Everyman." Other events,
phrases, objects point to the struggle with evil:
when Brown says, "What if the devil himself should be
at my very elbow!" the traveler suddenly appears;
Goodman says, "Faith kept me back awhile"; the
stranger's walking stick has a snake carved on it and
looks alive.

The story seems to work best in class when the
allegorical reading comes out piecemeal but rather
fully and without nagging doubts. If it goes on long
enough someone in the class is bound to react,
relieving you of the responsibility. There are
bothersome details. Why does Faith wear pink ribbons?
What's the innocent Brown doing going into the woods
at night in the first place? Clearly, he's up to no
good, and he even feels guilty about it. So maybe he's
not quite so innocent, at least about himself. Why

does he undertake the meeting soon, but not immediately, after he's married? Why is it that Faith's participation in the rites is more crushing to him than his father's or even the preacher's?

Students are used to discussions in English class winding up talking about sex, and clearly that's where this one is leading. It might also lead to sexism, however, and this might be a good point at which to try to distinguish between what a story shows and its attitude toward what it is showing. If the "sin" has to do with sex and sexuality, and if the hero accepts his own share of sin, no matter how guilty he feels, but is traumatized by seeing his bride's complicity, does all that add up to a sexist attitude? Is the story sexist for showing it or antisexist for doing so?

This discussion might lead to an exploration of fiction as telling truth by lying. How can we take seriously, and treat as meaningful, for our own problems and experience, a story about Satan and witches and people who lived a couple hundred years ago and had problems other than our own? It might be appropriate to ask whether the story is acceptable simply as "allegory," as "message-bearing," or whether we are not more concerned with the questions it raises about human actions and attitudes than with precepts or adages that it might offer. If the time isn't right, you might want to come back to this story (or assign it for the first time?) just before dealing with A Hunger Artist.

Shirley Jackson   The Lottery (p. 145)

The story is justifiably a favorite with anthologists, high school and university teachers, students, nearly everyone. A good many students will have read it and even studied it before. There's no need to engage student interest, nor much need to spur discussion. The trouble I often have is restraining students from interpreting symbols, extracting allegorical meanings, making assumptions, without paying close attention once more to the concrete detail. So I usually begin with more earthbound details like focus and voice or suspense. Sometimes I first try to get students to describe just where "the camera" is--from what point the narrator is viewing the proceedings. The focus once established, I ask just what the voice suggests about the (nonspatial) relationship of the narrator to the villagers. But I often try to approach the story from the point of view of expectations, of mystery or curiosity, of wanting to know what happens next--as in, say, The Most Dangerous Game.

Ask the students to look at the story from the first sentence. Where is it that anticipation is aroused? Of course the title arouses a bit of suspense, but an ordinary village drawing does not seem to hold out much promise. (If there are students who have not read or been told about the story before, they might be asked to stop reading after each paragraph and describe their expectations of what's to happen next. I've found that it takes a good many paragraphs before any real sense of expectation emerges.)

Another quality of the first sentences and paragraphs may at first seem puzzling: in some ways, they seem to discourage expectation. They are flat, somewhat colorless, matter-of-fact. The focus is dramatic, almost as if the narrator were a member of an audience looking at a play. We get into no one's mind or emotions: in fact, there don't seem to be very many emotions at first. The lottery, the only possible source of anticipation, is equated in the fourth paragraph more or less with square dances and Halloween programs, not a very exciting prospect. Students often testify either that the very absence of suspense creates suspense (as absolute silence does sometimes on the sound track of a film) or that the slow, somewhat ominous pace makes them pay attention to each detail, question it, and wonder what's going on. The latter are usually the first to try to wrench meaning from the text.

The flat tone will prove useful and effective later in the story. The revelation of the nature of the lottery is horrible, and the details, especially little Davy Hutchinson's being given pebbles to throw at his mother, make the scene almost unbearable. But the villagers treat it as routine (which may have something to do with what the story is saying) and the prose too is routine and dispassionate.

This might be a good point at which to discuss understatement and how it can create intense emotional effects. The flat, almost wholly unfigurative language and dramatic objectivity, along with the "static" structure which does not throw our anticipation forward in any definable way, slow us down, make us try to put the pieces of the story together to find out what's going on and, almost inevitably, what it "means." Shirley Jackson herself denied that she had any particular meaning or any meaning at all in mind while she was writing it, and professed to being somewhat bemused and amused at all the interpretations others had of the story. Whatever might have been her intentions, there is an air of meaningfulness in the story. It may or may not be specifically--and surely is not exclusively--about Puritanism, the scapegoat, man's inhumanity to man, the dehumanizing effect of ritual or custom, etc. It seems to partake of all these meanings but to limit itself to none. It creates a new meaning, a "lottery"-type experience, which seems to stand for a kind of human communal activity for what there is no other satisfactory name. That is what I mean by a symbol, or symbolic--something that cannot be paraphrased, something that has areas of meaning or implication (a term I prefer to "levels," because many of these meanings interpenetrate and do not seem parallel or on different levels at all), implications and meaning that cannot be paraphrased or conveniently separated from the particulars of the work. This is a difficult concept to get across. It may seem to some rather mystical or fuzzy or even a dodge, but how can one otherwise explain the coexistence of meaning and no-meaning? the appearance of meaning without satisfactory paraphrase? the multiple interpretations of literary works? Allegory, I suggest, does have paraphrasable meaning, and may have multiple meanings or levels of meaning, but not all complex, suggestive works, like The Lottery or Wuthering Heights or Moby-Dick can be read as allegories without woefully reducing their power and richness. The best way I've found to get this concept across convincingly is to let the students offer competing readings, preferably in papers, so that they must pin themselves down. If three, four, or, even better, five competing and convincing readers come forth, and if argument carries the class no closer to consensus, you might spring either Shirley Jackson's statement from Come Along with Me, or just raise the question of how we can solve such an interpretive problem and decide which of the several convincing interpretations is the interpretation. Is it necessary to have an interpretation? Can two be true? three? What does it mean if a story can mean two things or three?

Questions for Classroom Use

1. With what expectations do you begin the story? Are there any elements in the first paragraph that seem aimed at heightening your expectations? at lessening them? Are you suspicious of those that seem to divert or lessen your expectations? What is the net effect of such "nonsuspenseful" details? Are there details that you would expect here or in the next few paragraphs that are missing? How does the absence of expected detail affect your expectation? The procedures of the lottery are described in great detail. What is missing? Are you aware that something

is missing upon first reading? When do you become suspicious? When did you first suspect that the "prize" would not be entirely pleasant? What specific expectations did you have during the drawing? Were you wishing that some particular character would win? that one or more specific characters would not win? Were you concentrating on who would win or what the prize would be or both? When you discover the winner and the prize, what earlier details do you recall? Did you feel any urge to reread the story?

2. Are the attitudes of the people in the crowd during the drawing understandable at the time? later? When you first discover the outcome of the lottery, how do you expect the others to react? How do you explain their reactions on first reading? later?

3. How would you describe the focus of narration? the voice? tone? What do these contribute to your expectations or interest? There seems to be a discrepancy between the tone and what we ultimately learn is being described. What examples of this are most glaring? Do these operate to decrease or increase the horror? Compare the effects here with those of a horror film or TV show you have seen recently. Can you generalize from this comparison the relative effects of overstatement and understatement or direct and indirect presentation of horror? Do overstatement and understatement or direct and indirect presentation imply something about the audience or the writer's expectations about his audience? How are the issues involved in the direct presentation of the horrible related to those involved in pornography?

4. Where (in what part of the country) does this story take place? What evidence do you have for knowing the location? What values or attitudes do you associate with that part of the country? What do these associations have to do with your understanding or interpretation of the story? How precise can you be in defining what the story says about human nature? Does the fact that you cannot be more precise--or that other readers can have rather different interpretations--make the story more or less meaningful?

5. Do you believe this story? Though it is hard to believe that such a lottery ever took place, that the story is even probable, much less factual, what kind of "truth" may there be in such a story? What does this suggest about the nature of all fiction (sometimes described as "telling the truth by lying")?

Flannery O'Connor   The Artificial Nigger (p. 151)

The "artificial nigger" is the central symbol of the story as well as its title. I would begin with

the title but not the symbol. I have great difficulty
with the final word of the title and prefer to refer
to this piece as "the Flannery O'Connor story." But I
think you have to put the snake on the table early on
and confront the offensive word and the racial and
social attitudes of the protagonists. Despite the
word, I believe it is easier to deal with racism here
than in A Rose for Emily where it is muted, for here
the voice is clearly separated from the values of the
characters and speaks from a higher educational,
religious, social, and presumably moral plane. If
anything, the issue is not whether the voice or
narrator shares the values of the protagonists but
whether it is too "superior," too condescending.
Perhaps because I am teaching at a once-segregated
private Southern university with all too few black
students--I rarely have more than two blacks in a
class of eighteen--I feel it imperative to get the
racial issue, dirty words and all, out in the open.

     It sometimes seems best to approach symbol in
this story indirectly, discussing the story first in
terms of its action or as an initiation story and
attacking symbolism only when you get to the
"artificial nigger" itself.

     Who is initiated in this story, and into what
truth is he initiated? This question might arouse
some initial differences of opinion and get the class
going. It's worked best for me when I've been able to
get each "side" to present its whole reading
positively rather than in dismissing the other. If
the discussion begins with Nelson, his initiation can
be related to the fallen idol theme, either simply in
terms of the story or in conjunction with Tanhum. The
boy, so contentious and independent at first, is
impressed even on the train by his grandfather's
greater knowledge and experience, and is shaken by
his early experiences in the city, so that despite
himself he takes his grandfather's hand and accepts
him as guide. Then he is betrayed and disillusioned.
He does not remain gloomy for the rest of his life
like Goodman Brown, nor does he separate himself
permanently from his betrayer, however: the
artificial nigger (the implications of which had
probably best be held off this early in the
discussion) brings them together. Nelson does retreat
in another way: he vows never to go to Atlanta again.
This would seem a convincing reading: the pattern of
the initiation story is clear and the theme and
definition of initiation fairly traditional--even the
youth of the protagonist would help the argument.

     The other "side," arguing that the grandfather
is the initiated, will surely point out the early
passage describing the two as looking almost the same

age. Though he may know more than Nelson, the grandfather is clearly at a loss in the city, and indeed gets lost. His initiation is also occasioned by his betrayal of his grandson; here the fallen idol is himself--he learns his own capacity for sin (the first time this aspect of initiation appears in the anthology but a prevalent one in initiation stories). He needs to be forgiven, needs mercy, and, here again, it is the artificial nigger that makes Nelson's reconciliation to his grandfather, his forgiveness possible.

It might be a good idea to get all of this out before getting into the religious dimension of the story. Like Young Goodman Brown this is, clearly, a religious story; Brown is more or less Old Testament-oriented, as it were, whereas this is a New Testament story; the other stresses the Fall, but this stresses redemption. The first story is more directly religious; this one could be summarized without mention of religion--you might be lucky and have someone in class summarize it without mentioning religion. Perhaps the place to begin the discussion of this aspect of the story and its symbols is its last three paragraphs: the middle one of these is most explicit; the first sets up the rural scene as surrounded by treetops "like the protecting walls of a garden," and the final paragraph describes the train disappearing "like a frightened serpent into the woods." You might want to go as far back as the third paragraph of the story with its references to Virgil and Dante to pick up this aspect of the story, or you might want to use this as a paper topic.

One question raised by the religious thread from Virgil to the end is whether Nelson's vow never to return to Atlanta is admirable or not. Is it a retreat from life or reality? Or, since the city, with its sewers and frightening creatures, is an Inferno, is the vow an eschewing of sin? Another question might be whether the religious element rises naturally from the tale or seems imposed upon it. Is this an allegory like Goodman Brown or a naturalistic story? Does the fact--if it is a fact--that some readers may read the story and like it, finding it funny and interesting and moving in a purely secular way, and that others may be able to show how almost all, if not all, of the details and much of the language can be explained in terms of a visit to Hell and the religious motif make this story better than the Hawthorne story, or worse, or have no evaluative relevance? This might be an occasion for discussing value judgments and how one arrives at them or defends them, and for addressing the proposition that "Everyone's entitled to his opinion."

There may be little agreement as to precisely what "the artificial nigger" means or even whether it "means" anything paraphrasable. In discussing the various possible readings, many of them related, I get a chance to distinguish between allegory and symbol. I usually opt for some quite literal reading: "The boy and his grandfather are brought together by their encountering a mystery. Their common incomprehension and rejection of the alien artifact unites them."

Questions for Classroom Use

1. What is the focus of narration at the beginning of the story? When does it first distinctly shift? Are there other shifts? Since the focus shifts from one centered consciousness to another, why is the entire story not presented omnisciently from the beginning? How are the shifting centers related to the action? to the theme?

2. How is language related to the focus of narration? When do you become aware of the irony in such passages as "age was a choice blessing"? How is irony related to the focus of narration? Do you feel there is a narrator who "looks down" on the simple characters from a superior, even if sympathetic, vantage point?

3. Who is initiated in the story? to what? If there is more than one initiation, are they reinforcing or contradictory or largely unrelated? How are Mr. Head's "youthful expression" and Nelson's "ancient" look related to maturity and initiation? How is racial "otherness" used as an aspect of initiation in this story?

4. Mr. Head's plan to get up before Nelson and "irk" him fails; Nelson's "superior sophistication" in having been born in the city is destroyed by his failure to recognize a black. What other victories and defeats are there for each? How do these define and enhance our expectations? How do they relate to initiation? Whose side are you on? Who "wins" in the end? How do you feel about the victory?

5. To what extent do the frequent religious terms and images elevate the theme from the particular to the universal or from initiation into maturity or reality to something that goes far beyond that? Does the story support or justify this larger meaning or does that meaning seem imposed?

6. What do you understand by the description of "the artificial nigger" as "some monument to another's victory that brought them together in their common defeat"?

7. What details or incidents do you find

humorous? Are you laughing with or at the characters?
Do any of their naive reactions to the city strike you
as illuminating or profound? Are any of the humorous
incidents pathetic too?

6 THEME

Leo Tolstoy <u>How</u> <u>Much</u> <u>Land</u> <u>Does</u> <u>a</u> <u>Man</u> <u>Need?</u> (p. 170)

What do you mean, Leo, that all a man (or person) needs is six feet of land (or seven--another title for the story is <u>Three</u> <u>Arshins</u> <u>of</u> <u>Land</u> and an arshin or archine is twenty-eight inches)? I guess that's true if all you're concerned about is dying and being buried (though come to think of it, you don't even <u>need</u> that--you could be cremated). But suppose you're interested in living. Then how much land does a person need? Probably more than forty acres and a mule, wouldn't you say? Probably less than the hundred square miles or so that Pahom seemed after--if by need you mean enough farmland to supply a family with food, shelter, a modest income. So it comes down to what you mean by <u>need</u>. This is the way a discussion might begin. Then again, it might not. But the point is that, though I made Tolstoy's theme and parable sound pretty simple, it is not quite so simple.

You might want to take off from this point on the difference between need and greed. The desire to have enough income to support a family in modest comfort is, no doubt, admirable; the desire to want more and more, to work yourself to death for material possessions is foolish, life-denying or -destroying, sinful. The last term is the most appropriate to the details of the story, for here the instigator of greed is the devil himself. You may want to ask your students to compare Tolstoy's devil, his disguises, and how he operates to Hawthorne's, and to see what conclusions about God or virtue or Satan and evil they can deduce from these figures. You may want to ask whether there is a secular equivalent to the devil here, whether property or income or materialism itself engenders the desire for more . . . and more. You may want to assign a paper comparing the need for wealth in this story and <u>Rocking-Horse</u> <u>Winner</u>. You may also want to ask your students if they have ever been guilty of avarice; it might make for a good personal essay, or even a short story, and it could bring the theme off the page for them. They may even be able to describe their own bedevilment.

Material wealth as land and need as burial plot work very well to define the distinction between material and spiritual need. Is there some way we can incarnate this distinction in terms appropriate to our materialist consumerism? How Many Ferraris Does a Person Need? somehow does not seem to make it. Perhaps an exercise or contest seeking such a term would bring home to difficulties and triumphs of finding precisely the right symbol to carry the meaning, suggestion, tone, and effect we want.

I asked in the text about the country-mouse/city-mouse discussion that begins this tale. You may want to use it to compare to the Rainsford/Whitney dialogue at the beginning of The Most Dangerous Game: both seem to set up the theme, and the women, like Whitney, disappear from the story. (Is the Connell story, then, also a parable?) You may want to point out, however, that the initial scene here actually causes the events that follow when Pahom, overhearing the conversation, tempts the devil. On the other hand, you may want to use it to show how Tolstoy universalizes the theme: the urban, commercial life is often compared unfavorably with agrarian life, the former being competitive and materialistic, the latter hard but serene and more "moral." This is not the comparison that is made in the opening scene of the story, the tradesman's life being described as temporarily--but only temporarily--more affluent, but riskier. The story locates competition, greed, and risk in the agrarian world and incarnates materialism in the most stable of material values--land (always, grandparents always say, the safest investment). Tolstoy makes materialism part of the human condition, not that of a particular kind or aspect of society, justifying the presence of cosmic evil, the devil, rather than "merely" social evil, as its agent.

Katherine Mansfield   Her First Ball (p. 182)

Like Young Goodman Brown, this is a rather subtle story that at first appears to be quite simple and obvious. The apparent initiation is rather conventional: time flies, youth is fleeting, or, as Leila wonders to herself, "Was this first ball only the beginning of her last ball after all?" Even eighteen-year-old students may respond to the passage of time-- remember how long summers were when you were nine?

Neither the story nor Leila stops there, of course. The music starts again, a young man asks her to dance, and she is once more enthralled. Youth may respond to thoughts of the ephemeral nature of our years, but it is swept up again by living in the moment as if that moment will live forever.

What seems to be the attitude of the story toward Leila's shaking off serious thoughts? Is she just an empty-headed girl incapable of serious thought? Is she

merely young and healthy--after all, what can be
gained by sitting around lamenting that time is
passing by? These questions may be interesting in
themselves, but they are also interesting in terms of
the focus and voice. We see in the story only what
Leila sees, and hers are the only inner thoughts we're
privy to. Clearly some of the language that is not in
quotation marks is nonetheless hers ("Oh, how
marvelous to have a brother!" for example). Are there
words and expressions that seem not to be hers? What
is the effect of keeping the story entirely or almost
entirely within her mind, eyes, and range of knowledge
and emotions? Does it help us to judge her responses?
Does it shift emphasis and attention to some aspect
other than the questions about youth and seriousness
raised earlier? This might be one of those stories in
which all or part may be rewritten from another point
of view--say, that of the elderly partner, or a more
"omniscient" view.

    You might want to use this story also to discuss
the possibility of distinguishing the attitudes of the
characters and the society from those of the author.
Why--some students, particularly some women students,
may ask--are male initiations in terms of hunting or
sailing or journeys or incidents in the "real" or
"outside" world, while female initiations are most
often presented in terms of such trivialities as
dances and other social occasions? Is it the writer,
male or female, who is to blame, or is this the
material his or her (sexist) society gives the writer
to work with?

William Trevor <u>Beyond the Pale</u> (p. 186)

    Sometimes I plunge right in and talk about the
theme or, more precisely, the title of this story: <u>How
Much Land Does a Man Need?</u> seemed virtually to
announce its parabolic nature and its theme in the
title; <u>Her First Ball</u> announces an initiation story
and, if not quite its precise theme, at least its
parameters; what about <u>Beyond the Pale</u>? There are
always some students who do not know the word "pale,"
so I have always found it wise to ask for a
definition. Okay: enclosure, boundary, and, as the
dictionary says, "now chiefly figurative, as, outside
the <u>pale</u> of the law." Also, "The (English) Pale," a
district around Dublin which was considered English.
In the Trevor story, Cynthia links the two meanings:
"'Murderers are beyond the pale . . . and England has
always had its pales. The one in Ireland began in
1395.'" The expression also suggests outside the
boundaries of polite society and its concerns: a few

Theme / 37

sentences earlier Cynthia has urged "that we should root our heads out of the sand and wonder about two people who are beyond the pale." Outside the cozy life of the southern English vacationing, bridge-playing foursome, then, outside the English Pale, is history and reality, the violent, lawless, agonizing struggle for freedom and justice, the Irish attempt to free Ulster from British rule.

But all this takes up at most two-thirds of the story, from the point at which Strafe, Dekko, and the narrator (Milly) return to the hotel from their walk and find everything in turmoil. Surely the first five or six pages (a third of the story), if there merely to establish scene and characters, make for a rather lengthy exposition.

Sometimes I subject this story to stop-and-go reading, assigning only this first third; I ask students not only to anticipate how it is going to develop but also to try to characterize it. The words they often use are "boring" and "too arty or highbrow" or "slow," words they would probably also use to describe most Edwardian or Georgian, Bloomsbury-type literature. This portion of the story does resemble a slightly vulgarized version of the slightly decadent, more than slightly refined or sensitive enclosed fiction of that type. Trevor seems to be defining the moral and spiritual nature of the modern English Pale mimetically. But he is taking his time about it, and for a while this may seem to be a tactical or aesthetic blunder.

When Cynthia rips into the blindness and deception in their ignoring Irish history and reality in their insular coziness, she does not stop there, however. She pulls their heads out of the sand also to make them look at the history and reality of their own useless, phony lives that they have disguised with a facade of social decorum and "civilized" behavior. The pale is not just the law or society but the barriers built within our own psyches, our refusal to face reality inside ourselves and our enclosed society as well as in the outside world. Is there a relationship between the two? Can society be healthy if individuals live lies? Can individuals be healthy and their lives whole if the law and society within whose pale they live are based on deception and narrow selfishness?

I am not sure whether this is essentially a political or psychological or moral story, and perhaps that is one reason why I like it: most of our experiences do not have neatly fenced-off areas called "political reality," "psychological reality," "moral reality"--there are no such pales.

This story may raise issues that some do not feel they have time to discuss in an introductory

course in literature, while others believe it is
precisely what introducing freshman or sophomore
students to literature is all about. Is history bunk
or a stream that runs through our lives and which we
ignore only at the risk of not truly living? How
concerned should we (must we) be with politics? world
news? If one function of literature is to offer us a
view of reality from a perspective not our own, is
not another to give us insight--or force us to look--
into our own lives? You will be able to think of many
more questions and phrase them more elegantly once
the can of worms called politics and literature is
opened.

I've often felt that sections like this were places where editors dumped the stories they wanted to include but didn't know what to do with, though I've known that the intention was supposed to be to give instructors a free hand with a certain number of stories and to demonstrate to students that a story in a chapter on plot is not necessarily a story that can be approached only through plot, etc. So now I'm faced with a dilemma: I want to shut up and let you get on with your teaching, and I want to make some helpful suggestions--and show that I at least think I know what to do with these stories. So let me have it partly both ways: for some stories I'll do my usual song and dance; for others I'll just tell you where in the text proper I was tempted to put the story.

The Secret Sharer is of course rich enough to work just about anywhere but I would teach it as an initiation story or in terms of focus: try to imagine it told any other way.

In earlier editions Chekhov's The Lady with the Dog was in the chapter on theme, but I could have put it in the chapter on character (Gurov's change from philanderer to lover would be interesting), or in that on setting (Moscow, Yalta), or symbol (sea, melon, fish).

A Hunger Artist obviously fits into the fantasy chapter but would also work very well with "Symbols" (I don't believe the meaning of the Kafka story is paraphrasable, by the way, despite the strong elements of allegory of art).

Flowering Judas might be taught with Boys and Girls--specifically female initiations--but it would be useful to teach in terms of setting or in a "political unit" with Beyond the Pale. It could also profitably be taught in the "Characterization" chapter.

A Conversation with My Father I wanted at one time or another to put in Chapter 2 because it is about endings and how endings often define the vision or meaning of a story.

I had thought of using Shiloh in the theme or symbol chapters, but it could also be used with Rocking-Horse Winner or Macomber among others as stories of marriage and its problems.

Kate Chopin   Beyond the Bayou (p. 207)

There is the distinct possibility that this story is going to get some of us some of the time in trouble in class. Earlier in the Guide I suggest that though the Hawthorne story may be showing a sexist society, by its very reflection of sexism it may be considered an antisexist story. In other words, a story's "picture" may not be the same thing as a story's "values." Here it may be more difficult to make that distinction: the picture is that of a racist society (though the admixture of French blood, language, and mores makes for some complications) and, while the values are in one sense universal, admirable, and uplifting--the triumph of love over fear, life over war and death--they also seem to reinforce racism through the use of the black mammy stereotype. American, and particularly Southern, white literature uses the stereotype rather extensively: see, for example, Nelson Head's response to the black woman in The Artificial Nigger for an oblique instance that by its very obliqueness suggests how widespread it is (for Nelson had not seen a black before he got on the train for Atlanta). Were there ever black mammies so loyal and loving and self-sacrificing, or is this a self-serving white myth, a version of experience seen only through a white perspective? If there were, if some black women were as devoted to their white charges as La Folle to Cheri, is this confirmation of the sterotype or is it another crime of slavery and exploitation--making the victim conform in her own heart and soul to the stereotype imposed upon her by society? Is there any relation, one way or another, of this stereotype to the "Momma comfort" in Toni Cade Bambara's surely un-racist un-Uncle Tom My Man Bovanne?

Is the stereotype necessarily or only accidentally racist? What of such all-white family-retainer-nurse-mother figures as Peggotty in David Copperfield who will not even marry while there is a chance of helping and protecting young David? To what extent is the type or stereotype related to social and economic class regardless of race?

Can we read, understand, appreciate a story within the terms of its cultural setting when that culture has values we hold reprehensible? Can we appreciate, for example, Nazi films or stories? Suppose the values in the story--like the power of love here--are admirable despite the cultural values? Prepare for some stormy weather.

As I suggested in the chapter, the geography in Beyond the Bayou is analogous to the psychological state of the protagonist and the moral values of the story itself. War, fear, death traumatize Jacqueline and turn her into La Folle, confining her within territory bounded by the bayou; love triumphs over fear and she crosses the bayou into life and the greater world. You might even call attention to how Chopin's palette reflects the theme: on this side of the bayou only the red and black of death and blood; on the other side there is still red and black but also white, gray, silver, blue, green.

The principle of "economy" in the short story, the principle that all details should be functional rather than arbitrary, is often illustrated by the Chekhovian statement that if there is a gun on the wall early in a story it has to be fired before the story is over. A gun shows up in the eighth paragraph. You might want to suggest the students' first reading stop there or after the next paragraph and see how many have the gun fired. Why does it seem so obvious here? Are there any false clues or red herrings (like the cough in <u>Amontillado</u> or the Gothic elements in <u>The</u> <u>Most</u> <u>Dangerous</u> <u>Game</u>)? Does the simplicity and symmetry of the story (father wounded-trauma/son wounded-cure) detract from the story? Does it give it the aura of folktale or myth? To what extent is the pleasure of the story derived not so much from plot or theme but from cultural details--the place, the people, the language--that are strange, real, convincing? In some classes an exercise in picking out effective or interesting details might lead to a discussion of how far our responses to a story are to the pattern or story as a whole and how far to discrete details.

James Joyce   <u>Araby</u> (p. 255)

Joyce seems to have been one of those writers for whom the short story meant the initiation story. His <u>epiphanies</u>, or moments when the reality or inner nature of things "shines forth," are almost the same as the "illumination" in most initiation stories. <u>Araby</u>, one might say, then, is a glaring example of the epiphany initiation. Brief, almost diagrammatic, and, one may hope, close to the experience of the students, there should be no initial difficulty in their reading or discussing this story, even though its perfect, almost chiseled form may seem static to some.

I like to start with the obvious here, and I have had some success in class in getting students to list the romantic elements--the paperback books, the boy's bearing his "chalice safely through a throng of foes" with tears and prayers, the name of the bazaar. Another list, a list of the "realistic" or antiromantic elements--the rusty bicycle pump and odor of ashpits, the drunks on the street, the uncle's stumbling homecoming, the banal banter at the

bazaar--will then graphically suggest the basic
contrast in the story. It is then not difficult to
show, from the end of the fourth paragraph ("my
foolish blood") to the final "vanity . . . anguish
and anger," the nature of the illumination, and its
relation to that contrast.

I like to begin something of a counterthrust by
asking whether the description of Mangan's sister
holding a railing spike and leaning toward the boy,
her hair, neck, hand, dress, petticoat illuminated by
the lamp is a romantic or realistic "painting."
(Curiously there's a rather similar piece of
chiaroscuro in The Dead, you will remember.) But the
issue soon becomes the relationship of focus and
voice. The focus is on the young boy, obviously; the
voice is that of the man who was that boy. Calling
his young self's blood "foolish," and describing his
walking through the market on Saturday in chivalric
terms, describing his desire as wanting to "veil" his
senses, and such alliterative inflated phrases as
"prayers and praises," suggest the emotional distance
between focus and voice, between the innocent and
initiated. But whose language is the final sentence
with its alliterative pairs "driven and derided,"
"anguish and anger"? And what of the rest of the
flexible, beautifully polished, rhythmic prose? I
guess what I'm getting at is that I feel there's a
great deal of affection for the boy-self in the
narrator, and a bit of nostalgia both for the lost
innocence and the intense--if foolish--feeling.
There's a much stronger streak of the Romantic in
tough-thinking Joyce, I believe, than most critics
admit.

I think, then, the tone of this story is not
simple, and this might be a good time to bring up the
subject of tone (which I don't do in the text). Also,
I like to call attention to the complexity of tone in
the story before I get into the personal experiences
of the class--so that the students don't feel too
uneasy about their own "foolishness" in puppy love.
But I can see that with some classes you might want
to get a personal paper first, take them to the edge
of embarrassment, or to the edge of that
sophisticated contempt that eighteen- or nineteen-
year-olds have for the childish actions of fifteen-
or sixteen-year-old puppies, and then spring the
complications.

D. H. Lawrence The Rocking-Horse Winner (p. 266)

This is an oft-anthologized story, one of
Lawrence's most popular. More than one person has

told me that it is the only story they remember from their introductory fiction class of ten or fifteen years ago. And yet (is that the right word?) it is not a typical Lawrence story.

Achsah Barlow Brewster remembers hearing Lawrence tell the story (quoted by Edward Nehls, D. H. Lawrence: A Composite Biography, Madison: University of Wisconsin Press, 1959, 3:43-44):

Out on the terrace of Quattro Venti [on the Isle of Capri], sitting in the spring sunshine, we were talking about the curse of money. He related his story of "The Rocking-Horse Winner," bringing money, but the little boy's death. The tale was told of a woman's inheriting a fortune, whereupon she bought herself a close collar of pearls; soon afterward a bee stung her on the throat, which swelled before the collar could be removed, choking her to death. Someone else recounted that a poor farmer inherited forest land which he sold for ten thousand dollars. When he was told it should have brought twenty thousand, he was so chagrined that he hanged himself on one of the trees. There seemed no end of such tales. Lawrence decided at once to write a volume of them under the title of Tales of the Four Winds [Quattro Venti] from which the proceeds should be divided equally among us, that the curse of the riches should be shared by us all.

The story was first published in Lady Cynthia Asquith's The Ghost-Book: Sixteen New Stories of the Uncanny (1926). The story might be read, then, as something of a jeu d'esprit, more at home among the collected ghost stories then in the collected Lawrence.

For just this reason, however, it may be a good story to use in order to discuss canon or the author's style or fingerprint. Here, in this most untypical story, Lawrence cannot help but write like Lawrence. The flat, fairy-tale-like or late-Tolstoy opening can be found in other Lawrence stories of the period, like Two Blue Birds. Vintage Lawrence too is the reality that lies beneath appearances, beneath words, even beneath actions: "Everybody else said of her: 'She is such a good mother. She adores her children.' Only she herself, and her children themselves, knew it was not so. They read it in each other's eyes." You might ask the students to compare this understanding with Mabel's sudden apprehension of Fergusson's love in The Horse Dealer's Daughter. (You might also want to ask them about their own experiences: whether there are things they know without words, despite appearances, underneath actions.) The theme of money or materialism versus love and life is also familiar in Lawrence's work, as is the perception that the lust for money is insatiable, and that even too much is not enough. Family tensions, deftly handled, are common in Lawrence--Odour, Sons and Lovers--even though the suburban setting may seem unfamiliar. The idea that this story is about masturbation for some reason has great currency--better not to inquire the reasons, perhaps. Riding even a rocking-horse may, it is true, be assumed to involve a certain amount of genital excitation; Paul's frenzy may be translated sexually and getting the secret name of the horse may suggest for some sexual climax. Freudian reading of this story is a reading out of the story. That is, the masturbation is not in the story, part of the story, demonstrable in detail in the story: it is a translation of the details of the story according to another formula or system than that contained within the story. This may be legitimate if you want to talk about Lawrence's sexuality or attitudes toward sex conscious or, especially, unconscious. It may be legitimate, too, in trying to explain reader response. Readers may respond to this story because it parallels or embodies the rhythms or structures of masturbation; maybe that's why some students remember it more vividly than other stories they read at the time. But that's a study of responses and the reasons for them, conjectural and fascinating, and it seems to me that this is quite a different thing from saying that this story is about masturbation.

Questions for Classroom Use

1. If you did not know that this and the preceding two stories were by the same author, what internal evidence (elements, views, language within the story) might suggest it? How does this 1932 Lawrence story differ from his earlier ones? Describe the continuity and the change or development in his work, assuming these stories to be typical of that work at the time of publication.
2. Compare the opening sentences of the Lawrence stories. In what ways might the opening of this story prepare you for the surreal or supernatural events later in the story?
3. What expectations are aroused by what precedes the first dramatic scene? by the divulging of Paul's luck? by the "secret within a secret"? When did you first guess how Paul learned the names of the winning horses? When did you first begin to suspect the eventual outcome of the story? Why is Paul's mother anxious about him? What is implied about

feeling and common sense? Is Paul's mother's anxiety part of the realistic or of the supernatural aspect of the story? What are the implications? tone? emotional effect? of Oscar Cresswell's final remarks?

4. What is the focus of narration? How would you characterize or identify the narrator?

5. The "center" of Paul's mother's heart is cold and hard, she is incapable of love, but other people think she is a loving mother; she knows it isn't so, and she knows her children know it isn't so because they "read it in each other's eyes." What does this suggest about appearance or behavior and reality? about different kinds of reality? about different kinds of knowing? To what extent does this prepare you for the strange nature of the events that follow? How does the vagueness--for example, the absence of names--of the first page or so prepare you for those later events? How does the relationship between inner and outer reality here resemble or differ from that relationship in the other Lawrence stories? in The Lady with the Dog?

6. What kind of literal sense do you make out of the children's hearing the haunted house whispering? their seeing in each other's eyes that they all hear it? that the rocking-horse hears it? What does Paul's mother mean by luck? How does he interpret it? Why doesn't Paul want his mother to know he's lucky? What happens when he does tell her? What is the irony of Paul's claiming luck? What does the story imply about luck?

7. Why do the voices in the house get louder or more insistent after Paul's mother gets the five thousand pounds? What is the effect on Paul? What does the story suggest about money needs?

8. In what sense may this story be considered symbolic or mythic? If mythic, and if myth is social or communal, of what social group or community is this a myth? Compare it as myth to The Lottery. Compare the focus of narration, the kinds of detail and lack of detail, the sentence structure and diction, and the mixture of the real and the surreal in The Rocking-Horse Winner and The Lottery.

James Baldwin   Sonny's Blues (p. 305)

Students from Harlem will know; black students, especially those from a ghetto, will pretty well know; white students from wherever will recognize and will usually at least try to empathize with this story of black experience. The ghetto, drugs, and

jazz as a way out are more or less familiar to all
Americans of the last quarter of the twentieth
century. Blacks in college or university as well as
second- or third-generation Americans will understand
the narrator's uneasiness and guilt, as well as his
earlier aloofness and distance: he's made it, and
he's proud of it--and guilty about those he left
behind. A great many in each generation and in every
ethnic group ought to be able to empathize with the
narrator's plight. That the death of his child has
sensitized him with regard to his brother is a kind
of wound that makes us recognize our common humanity,
perhaps. The story is a relatively recent one; the
setting is familiar indirectly to all of us and
directly to a fair number; the emotions are
accessible.
    Can white readers _really_ understand it (can men
really understand women's stories involving "female
sensibility")? This is a question that is bound to
come up, and should, but it is difficult to avoid
having the discussion get to the point of "Can,"
"Can't," "Can," "Can't," either in an obvious or
subtle way. One way I've found to break the magic
circle is to ask to whom the story is addressed. Is
it aimed at whites, either as a plea for
understanding and sympathy or as an indictment? Is it
aimed at blacks, giving a voice to their long silent
experience and if so for what kind of response? Is it
directed to educated, more or less successful,
upwardly mobile blacks, both to show understanding
and sympathy for their plight and to remind them not
to abandon their brothers and sisters?
    I rather think the last, but not with real
confidence. There is little about white persecution
in the story, and that incident is narrated about the
somewhat distant past and is placed in the notorious
South. I must admit I was a bit more confident of my
reading before I looked up the cup of trembling
passage in Isaiah--should we read that to mean that
trembling and fury will be visited on whites ("them
that afflict thee")? or pushers? or is the full
passage not relevant?
    The story is placed where it is in the anthology
precisely to raise such issues, questions about
socio-historical context and its importance in
understanding as fully as possible the meaning, the
methods, the tone, and other aspects of fiction--even
conjectural questions about what students think
readers a hundred years from now will get and what
they will miss, or how this story might be read in
India or Australia. Such questions can still be raised
if the story is taught not in this place but in a
group of stories by blacks--My Man Bovanne--or stories

about blacks--<u>The Artificial Nigger</u>, <u>Beyond the Bayou</u>.
But this is a fine story about human relationships, no
more limited to racial issues (except perhaps by our
contemporary social context) than <u>Young Goodman Brown</u>
is to Puritans or New Englanders. It is also a story
with an intricate and significant time structure, and
could be profitably studied alongside <u>Macomber</u>. An
interesting study of the structure, in a paper or in
class, might involve the rearranging of the scenes of
this story into chronological order supplemented by
descriptions of what that order or other orders would
change in the meaning and effect of the story. (This
exercise will be particularly appropriate if there has
been some discussion of the elevating of the marriage
theme at least to the level of the hunting theme in
<u>Macomber</u> by disturbing the straightforward
chronological order, as I have suggested in the <u>Guide</u>
discussion.)

Finally, the last four paragraphs of the story
may be used to open up the question of the
transmutation of life or emotion into art, as a theme
of this story and an explanation of its title; as a
continuation of a discussion of Lawrence's
nonfiction, particularly biographical prose and his
stories; as a positive example of art enriching life
compared to the example in <u>The Real Thing</u>.

Questions for Classroom Use

1. How do the first sentences of the story
arouse and channel your expectations? When and how is
each expectation satisfied or disappointed?
2. How is the first-person narrator identified
or characterized in the first sentence? first
paragraph? first couple of pages? in the story as a
whole? How does this presentation resemble and how
does it differ from that of the first-person narrator
in <u>My Man Bovanne</u> or <u>The Real Thing</u>? How would you
argue that Sonny is the main character in this story?
that the narrator is? What do you learn about Sonny?
In what order do you learn these things? How is your
knowledge and judgment of Sonny controlled by the
narrator? How does he let you see more than his own
judgment? At what point are his judgment, the story's
judgment, and your judgment of Sonny identical or
nearly identical?
3. What evidence is there that this story is
aimed at a white readership? a black readership?
Would a white and black reader see the same things in
this story? To what extent do your own racial/
political views affect your evaluation of the story?
To what extent is this the result of the current
sociopolitical context and to what extent is this

built into the story?

4. Can you arrange the scenes in this story in chronological order? What is gained (or lost) in terms of expectation and understanding by the nonchronological ordering of the scenes of the story? Can you explain the rationale of the nonchronological arrangement? Why does the story go back to the time when the narrator was a little boy? to a time before he was born? What are the implications about the nature of truth or of human behavior in these flashbacks?

Gabriel Garcia Marquez   A Very Old Man with Enormous
        Wings (p. 328)

The best defense, we're told, is a good offense, so I like to be offensive in teaching Very Old Man and ask students whether they can take a story like this seriously. If credibility doesn't come up, I ask if they believe the story. Then, do they "believe" the people in Beyond the Pale or Boys and Girls ever really existed or if the events happened as they are told? With luck, we're off and running on issues like probability and telling the truth by lying. Why should a probable fiction be better or more serious or more valuable than an improbable one? Aren't they both, after all, fiction--false? Well of course you can learn about people and about life from probable fiction, but how often do you run into a very old man with enormous wings? But do you learn anything about Pelayo and Elisenda in general? about provincial culture and provincial Latin American culture in particular? about crowd behavior? about human response to the unknown or extraordinary? Indeed, you can argue, you may be able to learn more about response to the unknown here than in, say, The Artificial Nigger. There you know about the lawn statue and feel superior to Nelson and Mr. Head, but here the extraordinary man is as strange to you as it is to the villagers. (You may want to compare the Garcia Marquez story in class to Kafka's A Hunger Artist or have the two compared in a written assignment, with emphasis on how people on the whole are viewed and on tone.) This may be a good point to bring up once more the symbol: is the old man a symbol? As a symbol, if he is one, does he "stand for" something? if so, what? if not, can he still be a symbol? We're back to symbols as non-paraphrasable units of meaning.

As usual--or perhaps more than usual--you of course must be prepared to handle quite different responses and to bring them back to areas you want to discuss at this point in the course. If credibility doesn't come up right away you may want to listen for interpretations of what the old man stands for and begin with symbol and work around to meaning in terms of the way the people in the story act, etc. Or someone may begin by saying that what Garcia Marquez is doing is recounting a folk tale straight, as if the narrator is as credulous as the villagers and that it is a kind of patronizing tale whose subject is human credibility. How do we deal with folk tales? Do we dismiss them? interpret them psychologically or anthropologically? accept them as a vision of reality from an angle quite different from ours but more or less common to a significant number of people in the world?

At some point in class discussion the realistic (some would say disgusting) detail in the story is sure to come up. It's easy to dismiss this merely as a device for achieving credibility or willful suspension of desbelief--an evasive half-truth, I think. I'd rather think of the details as part of the imagination or vision of the story, as if Garcia Marquez had said to himself, "What would happen if a very old man with enormous wings were found here in the village?" and had then imagined the consequences as precisely as he could.

One hopes someone will mention the humor--the neighbor woman who knows everything about life and death and who identifies the old man as an angel; Father Gonzaga's testing him with Latin; the villagers' plans for him, including his being "put to stud in order to implant on earth a race of winged wise men." I hope you don't have to explain why such details are funny; or why funny details don't disqualify the story from serious consideration.

Rather offputting realistic details, cruelty, greed, humor--what is it we feel reading this story? Does the mixture of real and fantastic have its analogue in the potpourri of emotions? And what, finally, do we feel about the old man--pity? fear? disgust? wonder? Do we want him to turn out to be a hoax? stay and play with the children and make Pelayo and Elisenda rich? die (to rid the world of monstrosity)? soar off into the sun?

One parting shot: how are we to take the subtitle, "A Tale for Children"?

Alice Munro   <u>Boys</u> <u>and</u> <u>Girls</u> (p. 333)

If, in what my students call "In the present day and age of these modern times of today," you have trouble getting a discussion started on this story, you'd better call for an investigation by the narcotics squad or hang up your mortarboard. Now if you just have trouble separating Bella from Elizabeth and Jane from Bill B. or Anita, and getting any of them to get back to Alice Munro's story, that's different.

In my perverse way, if I detect the proper intensity of seethe and the lid of indignation about to blow, I try to get their noses (in or out of joint) back into the text. I sometimes start them off with the second sentence: what's going on there with beautiful silver foxes versus killing and skinning them? Does this have anything to do with that more central killing, the killing of the horse, and with the more central concern of differentiation of the sexes? (No, no, don't get too far ahead of me. We'll talk about that issue more fully a little later.) And now the third and fourth sentences: the heroic calendars sent by fur companies (irony anyone?), and what does one of those calendars show? European heroes with "savages" serving as beasts of burden, all against a background of a rather hostile nature. Are we getting a picture where the narrator stands on social, political, economic issues? Any relation to. . . . Well, we'll get on to that in a minute.

Now, in the second paragraph, there's the girl's mother, who doesn't like the killing and skinning or the gruesome play of the hired man, or the smell. But the girl finds the smell "reassuringly seasonal, like the smell of oranges and pine needles." How could she associate those? Would this be the time to begin to talk about "innate" and "learned" or "acculturated"? The "feminine" responses of the mother and the "masculine" responses of the girl here and through much of the story may be looked at in these terms, mightn't they?

It might be impossible to keep "the issue" out of the discussion, but one good written or oral exercise might be character descriptions of the mother and of the father, of Laird, of the hired man. Can the students sketch the character of the narrator as a girl as well? An alternative assignment would be an analysis of the relationship between the girl and her father, the girl and her mother, her brother. You might want to call attention as well to the age as well as sex division, to child versus grown-up and the narrator's perception of grown-up versus child.

But sooner or later, and quite properly, the discussion will turn to the subject indicated in the title, the subject that dominates even if it does not exclude other subjects in the story. This may be a good story in which to stress "development" or the sequential and temporal ordering of the material, for the first and second halves of the story may suggest different emphases, and to "spatialize" the story or take evidence without regard for its place in the story may be misleading. To show the differences, you might want to ask the students to look at the contexts and implications of the two appearances of the phrase "only a girl." How do the students read the final paragraph of the story? You might want to to call attention to the narrator's differing roles in her earlier and later dreams. The turning point comes when she is eleven and involves the horses, yet that section is introduced by "I have forgotten to say what the foxes were fed." How could so significant an element in the story be "forgotten"? There would be no initiation story--at least not in these terms--without the horses, you might suggest. What kind of a story might it have been? You might point out that the trigger to the memory is the father's bloody apron, as if she was just remembering her childhood up to that point. you might ask the students whether this suggests anything about the older narrator's--the voice's--attitude toward the innocence of her childhood (the first part of the story), and toward her initiation into youth if not adulthood. Do these attitudes tell them anything about why certain details were included in the first part of the story, why they were treated the way they are there and why quite different details are selected and why they are treated quite differently in the second half of the story?

There is no sense denying the force of theme in determining much of the content and structure here, so I find it just as well to get it out on the table--though not necessarily first. You might want to ask in what sense the characters are representative: Father, Mother, Little Brother, Average Male, Girl? Do the students see any thematic relevance in the characterizing of the two horses? Would the girl have opened the gate wide for <u>Mack</u>? Is there any wider than sexist theme implied by the burdened savages, by Henry's Stephen Foster song, by the slaughtered foxes and horses?

Still, you might want to ask what degree the particulars of the story transcend the theme in interest and import. Are the details of fox farming and of life in rural Canada only interesting in their thematic implications? (You might here want to relate childhood and rural life--innocence/Eden/garden--as a common American theme.) Putting up the curtain between her brother's bed and hers may have thematic import, but are all the specific details of the unfinished upstairs bedroom, its contents, the

children's superstitions about security, their songs
interesting only in terms of the theme? (And, by the
way, to what degree is "boys-and-girls: childhood"
just as good a rendering of the implications of the
title, as "boys-versus-girls: sexism"?) Why does the
girl put her brother on the rafter in the barn,
endangering his life? How is it similar and how quite
different from the freeing of Flora?

What is the nature of the initiation in the
story? You may want to ask your students to compare
this story to <u>Araby</u>, perhaps with the handle of
romance-of-childhood versus realism-of-maturity, and
with some attention to the prose and use of detail.

Biographical Sketches

JAMES BALDWIN (1924-   )

Perhaps the leading literary spokesman for the American black man, Harlem-born Baldwin, long a resident of France, first attracted critical attention with his novel Go Tell It on the Mountain (1953), which dealt, somewhat autobiographically, with religious awakening (Baldwin was a minister at fourteen but later left the church). A novelist of distinction, short story writer, and dramatist, he is also an outstanding essayist, his best-known nonfiction prose being The Fire Next Time (1963). The most recent of his six novels is Just Above My Head (1979).

TONI CADE BAMBARA (1939-   )

Born in New York, Bambara received a B.A. from Queens College (1959), studied in Florence and Paris, and earned an M.A. from City College of the City University of New York (1964). She has been a dancer and teacher, as well as an editor, critic, and writer. Her work includes two collections of short stories, Gorilla, My Love (1972) and The Sea Birds Are Still Alive (1977) and a novel, The Salt Eaters (1980).

AMBROSE BIERCE (1842-1914?)

The tenth child of a poor Ohio family, Bierce rose during the Civil War to the rank of major, was twice wounded and cited fifteen times for bravery. He stayed in the army for a time after the war, then was a journalist in California and in London. Already known as "Bitter Bierce," and the author of Tales of Soldiers and Civilians (1891--later and best known as In the Midst of Life) and another volume of short stories, Can Such Things Be? (1893), Bierce was further embittered by the death of two sons and divorce. He published The Cynic's Wordbook (later called The Devil's Dictionary) in 1906. At seventy he disappeared into Mexico, reportedly riding with Pancho Villa, and is presumed to have died there.

ANTON CHEKHOV (1860-1904)

Son of a serf who became proprietor of a general
store which, when Anton was sixteen, went bankrupt,
Chekhov became a physician and author of a handful of
classic plays and of hundreds of short stories which
changed the course of the genre. His first published
work (1880), a piece for a comic weekly, was written,
it is said, in order to earn enough money to buy his
mother a pie for her birthday. His first collection
of stories, The Tales of Melpomene, was published in
1884, the same year that he completed his medical
studies and went into practice in Moscow. The lung
disease from which he was increasingly to suffer had
already appeared the year before. In 1888 he finally
broke into the more prestigious monthlies with a long
tale, The Steppe, and for the next ten years
continued to write plays and numerous stories. It was
the newly founded Moscow Art Theatre company that
finally assured his success as a dramatist, however,
when it performed The Sea Gull in 1898 (a play that
had failed two years earlier), Uncle Vanya
(previously published) the next year, Three Sisters
in 1901, and The Cherry Orchard in January 1904, six
months before his death at a German health resort. He
had continued during the 1890s to write short stories
and nonfiction for weeklies and monthlies and to
publish collections of short pieces. Around the turn
of the century his collected works appeared in ten
volumes. He was diffident about the immense success
of his works, thinking they would scarcely outlive
him, and despite that success he never forgot his own
humble origins, his early poverty and struggle for
education, and the plight of those who had not been
able to escape such conditions.

KATE CHOPIN (1851-1904)

The St. Louis-born Kate O'Flaherty in 1870
married Oscar Chopin and moved first to New Orleans
and then to a Louisiana plantation. Her two volumes
of short stories, Bayou Folk (1894) and A Night in
Acadie (1897), were for a long time dismissed as mere
tales of "local color." Recent attention to her short
novel The Awakening (1899), which treats sex and
marriage from a woman's point of view, has led to
renewed interest in and reassessment of her other
works.

RICHARD CONNELL (1893-1949)

At sixteen, Connell was city editor of his native Poughkeepsie News-Press, and editor of both The Daily Crimson and The Lampoon at Harvard (class of 1915). After World War I, he left his New York job as advertising editor to become a freelance writer, traveling to Paris and London and finally settling in Beverly Hills, California. His works include the volumes of short stories, The Sin of Monsieur Pettipon, Apes and Angels, Variety, and Ironies, and his novels, Mad Lover, Murder at Sea, Playboy, and What Ho!

JOSEPH CONRAD (1857-1924)

Jozef Teodor Konrad Nalecz Korzeniowski was born in Berdyczew, Polish Ukraine; at five he accompanied his parents into exile to northern Russia and later the district near Kiev and was left an orphan at eleven when his Polish-patriot father (and translator of Shakespeare and Hugo) died in Cracow, his mother having died four years earlier. Before he was seventeen he was off to Marseille, making three trips from that port to the West Indies as an apprentice seaman. After some veiled troubles in France, involving gambling debts and an apparent suicide attempt, he sailed on a British ship, landed in England in 1878, and spent the next sixteen years in the British merchant service, rising to master in 1886, the same year in which he became a British subject. In 1890, through relatives in Brussels, he got a job on a boat that siled up the Congo, the basis of the trip described in Heart of Darkness. He began writing in 1889 but did not publish his first novel, Almayer's Folly, until 1896, the same year he married and Englishwoman, Jessie George. Though a successful writer, he was not truly popular or financially independent until the publication of Chance in 1912-13. Among his major novels are The Nigger of the "Narcissus", Lord Jim, Nostromo, and Victory.

WILLIAM FAULKNER (1897-1962)

Perhaps the greatest of twentieth-century American novelists, William Faulkner spent almost his entire life in his native Mississippi. He joined the Royal Canadian Air Force in 1918 and in the mid-1920s lived briefly in New Orleans--where he was encouraged by Sherwood Anderson but was contemptuous of the literary crowd; he then spent a few miserable months as a clerk in a New York bookstore, and, in 1925,

took a long walking tour in Europe. In later years he
made serveral visits to Hollywood, writing for the
films, and spent his last years in Charlottesville,
Virginia. His works include The Sound and the Fury,
As I Lay Dying, Light in August, The Hamlet, and Go
Down Moses. Many of his works are interrelated by his
ficitonal Yoknapatawpha County and the reappearance of
characters or families from work to work. He received
the Pulitzer Prize in 1954 (for A Fable) and in 1950
the Nobel Prize for Literature.

GABRIEL GARCIA MARQUEZ (1928-   )

        Writer of novels, short stories, and
screenplays, Garcia Marquez was born in Colombia. He
studied law at the University of Bogota and then
worked as a journalist in Latin America, Europe, and
the United States. His first published novel, Leaf
Storm (1955, translated 1972), is set in the
fictional small town of Macondo, based on his
childhood home where he had heard the myths and
legends which influence his work. His most famous
novel, One Hundred Years of Solitude (1967,
translated 1970)--which has been translated into more
than thirty languages and has sold more than ten
million copies--also covers the moral decay of
Macondo which serves as a microcosm of many of the
social, political, end economic problems of Latin
America. Among his works are The Autumn of the
Patriarch (1975, translated 1976), Innocent Erendira
and Other Stories (1972, translated 1978), and
Chronicle of a Death Foretold (1981, tranlsated
1982). In 1982 he received the Nobel Prize for
Literature.

NATHANIEL HAWTHORNE (1804-1864)

        Born in Salem, Massachusetts, educated at
Bowdoin College, this great early American writer
supported himself from time to time in government
service; working in the cusom houses of Boston and
Salem and serving as United States consul in
Liverpool. His early collections of short stories--
Twice-Told Tales and Mosses from an Old Manse (from
which Young Goodman Brown is taken)--did not sell
well, and it was not until the publication of The
Scarlet Letter in 1850 that his fame spread beyond a
discerning few. His other novels include The House of
the Seven Gables (1851) and The Blithedale Romance
(1852), and his short stories were gathered in, among
others, Twice-Told Tales (1837, enlarged 1842) and

The <u>Snow-Image</u> <u>and</u> <u>Other</u> <u>Twice-Told</u> <u>Tales</u> (1851).

ERNEST HEMINGWAY (1899-1961)

Born in Illinois, Hemingway was first a
reporter, then an ambulance-service volunteer in
France and infantryman in Italy in 1918, when he was
wounded and decorated for valor. After the war and
more reporting he "settled" in Paris, where he knew
Gertrude Stein and Ezra Pound, among others. From
1925 to 1935 he published two volumes of short
fiction--<u>In</u> <u>Our</u> <u>Time</u> and <u>Death</u> <u>in</u> <u>the</u> <u>Afternoon</u>,
about Michigan and bull-fighting, respectively; two
novels--<u>The</u> <u>Sun</u> <u>Also</u> <u>Rises</u> and <u>A</u> <u>Farewell</u> <u>to</u> <u>Arms</u>,
about Americans in post-war Europe and the war
itself--and <u>The</u> <u>Green</u> <u>Hills</u> <u>of</u> <u>Africa</u>, largely about
hunting. He helped the Loyalists (the anti-Franco
forces) in the Spanish Civil War in 1936 and that
conflict is the subject of <u>For</u> <u>Whom</u> <u>the</u> <u>Bell</u> <u>Tolls</u>
(1940). He served as war correspondent in the Second
World War and from 1950 to 1960 lived in Cuba. <u>The</u>
<u>Old</u> <u>Man</u> <u>and</u> <u>the</u> <u>Sea</u> was published in 1952, winning
the Pulitzer Prize the next year. Hemingway was
awarded the Nobel Prize for Literature in 1954. He
committed suicide in 1961.

SPENCER HOLST

Well known in the literary underground, Holst
has published his short stories and poetry in
numberous periodicals such as <u>Mademoiselle</u> and <u>Oui</u>.
He has translated the work of German poet Vera
Lachmann and published several volumes of his own
writing, including two volumes of short stories,
<u>Language</u> <u>of</u> <u>Cats</u> <u>and</u> <u>Other</u> <u>Stories</u> (1971) and <u>Spencer</u>
<u>Holst</u> <u>Stories</u> (1976), a collection of imaginative and
humorous fables which play with reality and fantasy.

SHIRLEY JACKSON (1919-1965)

This San Francisco-born master of the neo-Gothic
was graduated from Syracuse University in 1940 and
married the famous critic Stanley Edgar Hyman the
same year. In 1961 she appropriately won the Edgar
Allan Poe Award. Among her works are <u>The</u> <u>Lottery</u>,
<u>Life</u> <u>Among</u> <u>the</u> <u>Savages</u>, <u>The</u> <u>Haunting</u> <u>of</u> <u>Hill</u> <u>House</u>,
and <u>We</u> <u>Have</u> <u>Always</u> <u>Lived</u> <u>in</u> <u>the</u> <u>Castle</u>.

HENRY JAMES (1843-1916)

Son of a writer, brother of the philosopher
William James, Henry entered Harvard Law School in
1862, after private study, art school, and study and
residence abroad. Thereafter his American home was in
Cambridge, Massachusetts, but he lived in London from
1876 until his death forty years later, having become
a British subject in 1915. One of the greatest of
American writers, James's fiction often centers on
the confrontation of Americans with Europe or
Europeans; he treats the two as moral- or value-
systems as much as nationalities. His practice and
his theory of fiction, set forth mainly in the
prefaces to his novels, dominated fiction criticism
for generations. Among his works are The American,
The Europeans, Portrait of a Lady, The Turn of the
Screw, The Ambassadors, and The Golden Bowl.

JAMES JOYCE (1882-1941)

    In 1902, after graduating from University
College, Dublin, Joyce left his native city for
Paris, only to return in April 1903 to teach school.
In the spring of 1904 he lived at the Martello Tower,
Sandycove, a site made famous by his great novel
Ulysses (1921). In October 1904 he eloped with Nora
Barnacle and left Ireland again, this time for
Triests, where he worked for the Berlitz school.
Though he lived abroad for the rest of his life, that
first abortive trip proved symbolic: in his fiction
the expatriate could never leave Dublin. We can
perhaps understand why a half-century ago Ulysses was
banned for a dozen years in the United States and as
long or longer elsewhere, but it may be difficult to
understand now why the volume of short stories,
Dubliners, in which Araby appears, completed in 1905,
was not published until 1914. Even The Portrait of
the Artist as a Young Man, dated "Dublin 1904,
Trieste 1914," had its difficulties, first appearing
in America in 1916. Though he published a play,
Exiles, and poems, the three works mentioned and the
monumental, experimental, and puzzling Finnegans Wake
(1939) are the basis of his reputation as one of the
greatest writers and innovators of the twentieth
century.

FRANZ KAFKA (1883-1924)

    Born in Prague, Kafka earned a doctorate in law
from the German University in that city and worked
for a workman's insurance company. Emotionally and
physically ill for the last seven or eight years of

his rather short life, he died of tuberculosis in
Vienna, never having married (though he was twice
engaged to the same woman and lived with an actress
in Berlin the years before he died) and not having
published his three major novels--The Trial, The
Castle, Amerika. Indeed, he had ordered his friend
Max Brod to destroy them and other works he had left
in manuscript. Fortunately, Brod did not, and not too
long after his death, Kafka's work was world famous
and widely influential; he is now recognized as one
of the greatest and most important writers of the
first half of the twentieth century.

D. H. LAWRENCE (1885-1930)

     His father a coal miner, his mother middle
class, young "Bertie" Lawrence won a scholarship to
Nottingham High School when he was thirteen but had
to leave school a few years later when his elder
brother died. He worked for a surgical-appliance
manufacturer, became a pupil-teacher, and attended
Nottingham College, where, in 1906, he earned his
certificate; he left Nottinghamshire for Croydon,
near London, where he taught school. When, in 1911,
his first novel, The White Peacock, was published, he
left teaching to devote his time to writing. The next
year he eloped to the Continent with Frieda, wife of
Professor Ernest Weekley and daughter of Baron von
Richthofen; in 1914, after her divorce, they were
married. During World War I both his novels and the
fact that his wife was German gave him trouble: The
Rainbow was published in September 1915 and
suppressed in November; in 1917 he and his wife were
ordered away from the Cornish coast, suspected of
spying for the Germans. Understandably, in November
1919 the Lawrences left England. Their years of
wandering began: first Italy, then Ceylon and
Australia, Mexico and New Mexico, then back to
England and Italy. His troubles with publishers were
not ended by his exile, however: Women in Love was
published in a subscription edition in New York in
1920, and Lady Chatterley's Lover in a similar
edition eight years later, but even that was not
enough to stem the outrage that lasted for more than
a quarter-century after his death; even a volume of
his poems was seized in the mails. Through it all he
suffered from tuberculosis, the disease from which he
finally died, in France. His other major novels
include Sons and Lovers, Aaron's Rod, and The Plumed
Serpent.

DORIS LESSING (1919-   )

     Born in Persia, Lessing lived for twenty-five
years (1924-49) in Southern Rhodesia (now Zimbabwe)
before moving to England, where very soon thereafter
her first novel, The Grass Is Singing, was published.
She has since published voluminously. Her best-known
novels are The Golden Notebook (1962) and the five
Martha Quest novels, Children of Violence, published
between 1952 and 1969. She has published as well at
least eight volumes of short fiction, including A Man
and Two Women (1963) and The Temptation of Jack
Orkney and Other Stories (1972), and written seven
plays, four television plays, verse, and essays. Her
work is notable for its range and variety, some of it
set in Africa, a significant portion of it political
(she was once a Communist), and much of it probing
the nature of the life of a woman in modern society.
She has recently turned from the novels in her
cosmological work called collectively Canopus in
Argos: Archives to two novels first published under a
pseudonym but now collected under her own name, The
Diaries of Jane Somers (1983-84), and to her most
recent novel, The Good Terrorist (1985).

KATHERINE MANSFIELD (1888-1923)

     Born in New Zealand, educated at Queen's
College, London, an accomplished cellist, Mansfield
published four major volumes of short stories--Bliss
(1920), which established her reputation; The Garden
Party (1922); The Doves' Nest (1923); and Something
Childish (1924). She lived with John Middleton Murry
for several years before marrying him in 1918; with
Murry and D. H. Lawrence she founded a review, The
Signature. She died of tuberculosis in France.

BOBBIE ANN MASON (1940-   )

     Mason has written for Movie Stars, Movie Life,
and T.V. Star Parade, earned a doctorate, and taught
English. She has been awarded a Guggenheim Foundation
Fellowship, has had stories in Best American Short
Stories in 1981 and 1983 and won the Pushcart Prize
for fiction in 1983. Shiloh and Other Stories (1982)
was her first collection and earned her nomination
for both the National Book Critics Circle Award and
the American Book Award as well as winning the Ernest
Hemingway Foundation Award. Her first novel, In
Country, appeared in 1985.

GUY DE MAUPASSANT (1850-1893)

Born Henri Rene Albert in Normandy, at sixteen
"de Maupassant" was expelled from a Rouen seminary
and finished his education in a public high school.
After serving in the Franco-Prussian war, he was for
ten years a government clerk in Paris. A protege of
Flaubert, during the 1880s he published some three
hundred stories, a half-dozen novels, and plays. With
Chekhov, he may be said to have created the modern
short story; his reliance on plot, plot twists, and
sometimes heavy irony became facile in the hands of
his followers and has somewhat diminished his own
reputation the past quarter-century and more. His
life ended somewhat like one of his own stories: he
died in an asylum, of syphilis.

ALICE MUNRO (1931-   )

A native of Canada, Munro began publishing short
stories while she attended the University of Western
Ontario. Much of her fiction grows out of her
southern Ontario childhood memories. Her first book,
a collection of short stories called Dance of the
Happy Shades (1968), won a Governor General's Award.
Munro has written a novel, Lives of Girls and Women
(1971), and three other short story collection,
Something I've Been Meaning to Tell You (1974), Who
Do You Think You Are? (1978, published in the United
States as The Beggar Maid in 1979), and The Moons of
Jupiter (1983).

FLANNERY O'CONNOR (1925-1964)

Savannah-born Flannery O'Connor received an A.B.
from the Georgia State College for Women and an
M.F.A. in writing from the State University of Iowa
(1947). Her first novel, Wise Blood, was published in
1952 and her first collection of stories, A Good Man
Is Hard to Find, in 1955. She was able to complete
only one more novel, The Violent Bear It Away, and a
second collection of stories, Everything That Rises
Must Converge, before dying of an incurable illness
in Milledgeville, Georgia. Her reputation as one of
the truly important writers of her generation has
continued to grow since her untimely death. A
collection of her letters, edited by Sally Fitzgerald
under the title The Habit of Being, appeared in 1979.

GRACE PALEY (1922-   )

A native New Yorker, Paley studied at Hunter College and New York University. She currently teaches literature at Sarah Lawrence College. Her short stories have appeared in leading magazines as well as in three collections, The Little Disturbances of Man (1959), Enormous Changes at the Last Minute (1974), and Later the Same Day (1985).

EDGAR ALLAN POE (1809-1849)

Poe's actor father deserted his wife and son when Edgar was less than a year old. His mother died before he was three, and he and his baby sister were separated by being taken into different families. The Allans (who gave Poe his middle name) moved to England in 1815 where Edgar had his early schooling. His brief stay at the University of Virginia--good grades, bad hangovers--ended after he quarreled with his foster father over money. In 1827 he paid to have a volume of poems published in Boston (his birthplace), and a second volume appeared in 1829 in Baltimore (where he was to die twenty years later). Having served well for two years in the army, he was appointed to West Point in 1830 but apparently managed to have himself expelled within the year for cutting classes. Living in Baltimore with his grandmother, aunt, and cousin Virginia (whom he married in 1835 when she was thirteen), he began to attract critical notice for his writings, but made very little money. For the twelve years of his bizarre marriage (which some say was never consummated), he wrote, worked as journalist and editor, and drank hard. Not long after his wife died in 1847 he seemed to be straightening himself out when, on election day--October 3, 1849--he was found semiconscious near a polling place, dying four days later without fully regaining consciousness. Had he been drugged and hauled around to vote again and again? Or was he on another binge? It is testimony to the continuing fame of his works that they need not be named here.

KATHERINE ANNE PORTER (1890-1980)

Porter's life was long but her career as a writer of short stories and short novels was short. Her first volume, Flowering Judas, made up of stories that appeared in magazines in the previous decade, was published in 1930, her last (except for Collected

<u>Stories</u>, 1966, which added only earlier works), <u>The</u>
<u>Leaning</u> <u>Tower</u>, in 1944. She published one long novel,
<u>The</u> <u>Ship</u> <u>of</u> <u>Fools</u>, twenty-five years in the making,
but is at her best in shorter forms, where her
concision and precision of diction and style enable
her brilliantly to capture a character, a culture, or
chaos. A warning about reading <u>Flowering</u> <u>Judas</u> or her
other stories: "reviewers are much mistaken," she
said, "when they insist on identifying me with any
and every woman that appears in my stories. . . . I
am a considerably more complicated person than they.
They were not writers." Porter was awarded the Gold
Medal of the National Institute of the Arts in 1967.

MORDECAI RICHLER (1931-   )

    Born in Montreal, the son of working-class
Jewish parents, Richler attended Sir George Williams
University for two years and worked as a freelance
writer in Paris and London from 1952, returning to
live in his native Quebec only in 1980. His writing
is varied and includes short stories, essays,
screenplays, and novels. His <u>Cocksure</u> (1968) and <u>St.</u>
<u>Urbain's</u> <u>Horseman</u> (1971) won the Governor General's
Award and his own screen adaptation of his novel <u>The</u>
<u>Apprenticeship</u> <u>of</u> <u>Duddy</u> <u>Kravitz</u> (1959) was nominated
for an Academy Award in 1974. His most recent novel
is <u>Joshua</u> <u>Then</u> <u>and</u> <u>Now</u> (1980).

LEO TOLSTOY (1828-1910)

    Identify this novel: The hero is born into a
noble family, orphaned before he is ten, studies
Oriental languages, then law, then settles on the
family estate where he tries to improve the lot of
the oppressed workers, but they treat him with
suspicion. He serves in the army during the war,
returns home, founds a school, marries and writes two
monumental novels, masterpieces. But he isn't
satisfied. He finds his life, in his own words,
"absurd . . . a stupid and spiteful joke," and is
converted, first to his national religion, then to a
kind of "primitive" Christianity. He opposes the
military, capital punishment, persecution of the
Jews; he gives up alcohol, meat, and as much of his
property as his family will allow. He flees from
home--where his wife is trying to have him declared
incompetent--intending to enter a monastery, but dies
in a railway station en route. It's not a novel but
the life of Leo Tolstoy, author of <u>War</u> <u>and</u> <u>Peace</u>
(1863-69), <u>Anna</u> <u>Karenina</u> (1873-76), and, after his

conversion, <u>The Death of Ivan Ilyich</u> (1886) as well
as <u>How Much Land Does a Man Need?</u> and many other
stories, parables, and novels.

WILLIAM TREVOR (1928-   )

     Born William Cox in Ireland, Trevor lives in
England. He has been a teacher--chiefly in England
but including a stint at Armagh, Northern Ireland,
1950-52--and an advertising copy writer as well as a
sculptor (for which he won an award in 1953),
novelist--including <u>The Old Boys</u> (1964), <u>Lovers of
Their Time</u> (1979), and <u>Other People's Worlds</u> (1980)--
and short story writer. Many of his stories have been
adapted for BBC radio. His volumes of short stories
include <u>The Day We Got Drunk on Cake</u> (1972), <u>Angels
at the Ritz</u> (1975), and <u>Beyond the Pale</u> (1982); his
<u>Collected Stories</u> was published in 1983. He has won
the Hawthornden Prize (1965) and the Benson Medal of
the Royal Society of Literature (1978), and was named
Commander, Order of the British Empire, in 1979.

POETRY

Teaching Poetry

How to begin teaching poetry? The arrangement of the poetry section of The Norton Introduction to Literature suggests one way; in fact, it suggests a beginning, middle, and end for a unit on poetry-- moving from some of the simpler issues of interpretation to more complicated ones. Still, you have a lot of choices to make, for few courses offer enough time to raise all of the questions and problems that are built into the textbook. And probably no course offers enough time to discuss adequately all the works of literature in the text.

The first two chapters provide an introduction to some of the issues on students' minds when they begin a unit on poetry, and I hope that the discussion there will defuse for you some of the objections that students sometimes raise when they first face the serious study of poetry. For many students, the experience with poetry that you provide them will be the first serious exposure that they will have had, and choosing the right poems for them to study in detail is crucial.

At the ends of chapters 1 and 2, there are three different groups of poems, each centered on a particular subject. Which groups you choose to work with--and which poems within each group--will probably depend not only on which poems you like best and feel you can best explicate, but also on the particular background of your students. The poems on love and on mothers and fathers are perhaps the most accessible, although some of them are very complex as individual poems; the group can also be read fairly easily without getting into some of the more complex issues.

I like to wing it a little in the early class meetings, trying out three or four poems with students before committing myself completely to a syllabus (although that flexibility may not be possible in large, multi-section courses with a pre-set syllabus). But if you have flexibility, use it: Have your students talk the first day about what poems they have already read and liked; have them fill out a card on which they indicate how much formal training they've had and what their nonliterary interests are. With such information and with the experience of three or four class meetings, you will be in a better position to know which group of poems is best; and each offers enough good poems and sufficiently sophisticated issues in some of the poems to keep interested those students who may be ahead of the average in your class.

The poems at the end of chapters 1 and 2 are grouped by topic in order to give you a chance to do two things in class: (1) read individual poems closely in order to see what they say, what they do, how they work; and (2) compare poems that have one thing (similar subject matter) in common so that individual differences begin to show up very early, even before your students will have terminology adequate to articulate them fully. Each group contains a variety of modern and traditional poems, a sufficient variety to raise many kinds of questions for class discussion, and there are enough poems in each that you can skip any poems you don't like or would rather not discuss. I myself usually do at most two groups and I usually do fewer than half the poems in each group, changing the selection every time I teach the course. I raise some technical problems early (it's hard to get far without mentioning, for example, the questions of speaker or word choice), but I do it randomly as the issues come up in a particular poem, saving systematic discussion for later.

The seven chapters following the first two systematically introduce technical problems--speaker, setting, diction and word order, metaphor and symbol, structure, rhythm, verse form. Not every teacher will want to take up all these issues, at least not systematically, and in the chapters themselves I have tried to say the most basic and elementary things so that, if you like and if you have time, you can take up some more difficult problems in class, using either the examples I discuss in the chapter or the generous selection of poems at the end of each chapter. You may find, too, that you would rather choose some of your examples from elsewhere in the text (I often do that myself; I don't like to use the same examples every time I teach the course, and besides it is good for students to recognize that any poem can be used as an example of a lot of different things, that skipping around is an intelligent thing to do). I won't be offended either if you prefer to teach these chapters in a different order; I like to bring up the issues in this order because it works for me, but I've tried to make it possible for you to move the chapters around to suit yourself. Even when one of my comments looks back at another poem, it could just as easily look ahead. Raising an issue before you are really ready to discuss it--just warning your students that it

is there--is good pedagogy, I think. The relevant
section of the Glossary is numerically parallel so
that, for example, you can refer your students to
section three of the Glossary to review terminology
after you have taught chapter 3 on the question of
"speaker."

I have put quite a number of poems in a
"Further Reading" section at the back, taking them
out of groups and categories altogether. I hope
that here you will find some poems you want to
teach in one unit or other early in the course; the
"open" grouping is intended to suggest more
flexibility and invite you to shop for poems you
want to teach in a particular way. But there's
another reason for the large open group too. Many
of these poems are particularly challenging and
could well be appropriate at the end of the course
when your students will have acquired a variety of
skills. It's not a bad idea to see if they can do
"everything" with a few of these poems at the end
of the course as a kind of review. It is a good
confidence builder.

Whether you make up your own syllabus or
conform to one already set, one of the toughest
decisions involves how to distribute class time.
Basically, the decision comes down to the question
of intensiveness versus extensiveness; you clearly
can't discuss as many poems in class if you do each
one thoroughly. Compromises are of course possible;
you can vary the pace depending on the difficulty
of individual poems, you can set up study questions
on poems you don't have time to discuss, you can
assign four or five poems for a given class meeting
and pick only one for discussion, you can have
exceptional days in which, if you usually discuss
one poem intensely, you instead teach briefly seven
or eight poems (or vice versa). It seems to me
helpful to retain some flexibility, perhaps even
putting "open" or "catch-up" days in your syllabus
or occasionally scrapping a planned assignment in
favor of something that has become crucial to the
class. I usually spend the better part of a class
on one poem, especially early on, but I almost
never (except for the first two or three class
meeting when I am emphasizing how much there is in
every poem and how closely one must read) assign
only one poem. Asking students to read one poem
five or six separate times probably involves noble
intent, but an assignment that consists of only one
poem (a few pages of reading at most) doesn't look
like much to any student and probably sets a bad
class expectation. Often I choose three or four
short poems for a day's assignment, discuss the

most difficult one in class, and either point to one or two specific problems in the others or (more profitably if there is time) ask students to raise questions that troubled them. The key to good class discussion is clearly good preparation (theirs as well as yours), and anything you can do to stimulate sensible preparation is a real help.

Getting the whole class involved in discussions seems to me crucial, but sometimes it is difficult, partly because some students seem to be shy of poetry and partly because others get excessively enthusiastic and sometimes want to dominate the discussion. It may take your whole bag of tricks to keep balance and order in the classroom, but you can help yourself somewhat by insisting on the kind of careful and precise preparation that will ask everyone to think deeply about certain problems before class. Sometimes this is best done by a last-minute, looking-ahead comment at the end of a class, sometimes by study questions handed out ahead of time, sometimes by quizzes, sometimes by assigning brief mini-reports to individual students for a future class meeting. Which ones to try depend upon the make-up of individual classes and upon particular opportunities and problems that arise, and I don't know any general rule to use except to keep a close watch upon the class dynamics, especially in the beginning.

One thing that does practically guarantee--at least in the long run--close attention to class discussion is the assignment of challenging and frequent papers. What you can do in this area--as distinguished from what you'd like to do--will of course depend on the size of your class and the number of weeks you have to devote to poetry. Papers almost inevitably get students to think deeply and formulate their thoughts and feelings articulately. I think it's especially important to assign papers early (I usually assign a very short one for the third class meeting), and I prefer many short papers to fewer longer ones; that way you can help students more quickly with problems, and they can have several chances to prove and improve their skills. Papers on one specific aspect of a poem-- papers that can be done in 400-500 words--still almost inevitably ask students to confront the whole poem, and I find that classes improve in liveliness after each paper--at least as soon as the initial disappointments wear off. Papers are, of course, time consuming for you; to be effective they deserve extensive comment on both good and bad features, and individual conferences are usually necessary. The ideal is probably a paper a week and a conference a week, but unless your class is restricted to a very small size, you will have to adjust the ideal to fit reality.

Wherever you begin and at whatever pace you proceed, it is almost always a good idea occasionally to sum up and occasionally to set up something for future use. If you begin as I do by holding back as much as possible on technical problems, you may nevertheless want to mention some terms as an issue emerges in a particular poem and perhaps sometimes assign (or point toward) a particular section in the Glossary or part of a later chapter. I like to give a sort of impression of disorder at first (so much to learn, so little time), and then do some summarizing when we formally consider a particular technical issue, often asking my students to look again briefly at poems we have already discussed. This tends to provide a cumulative feeling about learning, and if you can do it unobtrusively (without playing "What do I have hidden in my hand?" too crudely and obviously) it gives the class a relaxed flow and a quiet sense of direction.

A number of the suggestions that follow will (I hope) point you toward other strategies of putting things together; I have made quite a number of suggestions about ways of teaching specific problems, and you may wish to skim through the whole Guide before looking in more detail at the comments, suggestions, and questions on individual groups and individual poems.

Experiencing Poetry

A Gathering of Poems about Love

"Love" covers a multitude of tones and issues here, and I'd suggest that, if you decide to teach some poems from this group, you try to illustrate how different poems capture the many facets of feelings and thoughts that go with love relationships.

Many other poems in the book are also "love poems" in a broad sense. You might want to glance ahead at some poem you want to treat later in a different context (such as Marvell's To His Coy Mistress, p. 512, for example).

Theodore Roethke   I Knew a Woman (p. 368)

1. List all the sensual words and images. How specific are the visual references to feminine appeal?

2. The poem uses a number of unusual expressions and visual suggestions, e.g., "lovely in her bones" (line 1), "moved more ways than one" (line 3), "flowing knees" (line 18), "cast a shadow white as stone" (line 25). How does the poem get away with nonliteral visualization when its major effect depends on a physical sense of presence? What is the effect of each phrase in isolation? in context? Explain the complex reference to the movements of the Greek chorus (lines 6-9) and to mowing (lines 12-14). What similar "cerebral" comparisons occur elsewhere in the poem? How do they function?

3. Why does the speaker appear to mock himself and his helpless devotion to his lady? How do you respond to the speaker? to the lady he talks about? Compare and contrast the speaker in They Flee from Me (p. 372).

Audre Lorde   Recreation (p. 369)

If you are teaching this poem early in the course, your students may not hear the pun in the title, and you may need to point them to the theme of creation (lines 12, 17-18, 22) and re-creation; you may even help them learn what the original meaning of recreation is, a renewal or remaking of oneself.

Anonymous Western Wind (p. 370)

   What does the poem fail to tell us about the
situation? How does what is not said make the poem's
emphasis clear? What emotions of the speaker are
specifically isolated? How do the first two lines of
the poem relate to lines 3 and 4?

Sharon Olds Sex Without Love (p. 371)

   What syntactical irregularities in the poem
point to overpowering feelings on the issue of "sex
without love"? (Compare the way Jonson, in On My
First Son p. 366, indicates emotion through
interrupted rhythms.) Compare the attitudes
toward sex in this poem with those in Roethke's
I Knew a Woman, and Piercy's To Have Without
Holding (p. 371).

Sir Thomas Wyatt They Flee from Me (p. 372)

   1. What is the speaker's attitude toward the
"special" (line 9) lady of stanzas 2 and 3? Why does
she stand out from the others? How do the old loves
of stanza 1 relate to the attitudes expressed in the
rest of the poem? Which part of the poem uses the
most precise detail?
   2. What generalizations does the poem suggest
about feminine behavior? about masculine behavior?
Does the speaker seem conscious of the rationale of
his behavior? Are the generalizations stronger or
weaker as a result of his own actions and attitudes?

A Gathering of Poems about Mothers and Fathers

   All of the poems in this group consciously look
backwards, and memory is crucial to all of them. It
is interesting to see what objects and what people
the different poems pick out to dwell on in their
effort to find meaning in the past. All the poems
share in a quest for personal identity; many of them
look for meaning in the idea of family, ancestry, and
roots, and for many, some little thing, some small
detail, takes on major significance for the speaker.
   Students who don't relate especially well to
poetry often respond to these poems, perhaps because
the issues raised are ones that everyone thinks about
and they don't seem especially "literary" issues. It
may be worth letting your students do a little bit of

autobiographical analysis of their own memories, getting them to be conscious of what events and objects stick in their minds when they think about their childhood and their parents. If you want to put some emphasis on rhetorical strategies early in your course, this group provides a good opportunity because students can come quite close here to seeing themselves in the position of the poet--not a frequent opportunity. Get them to explain how they would make, in explaining themselves to others, a particular detail about their mother or father come alive.

Robert Hayden   Those Winter Sundays (p. 374)

What effect is gained by the decision to treat the early morning scene as a repeated ritual rather than as a narrative of an event? What is implied by "too" (line 1)? Why does the poem alternate between formal, restrained terms such as "chronic angers" (line 9) or "austere and lonely offices" (line 14) and more immediate emotive terms like "blueblack" (line 2) and "splintering" (line 6)? How is the contrast between present and past suggested?

A Gathering of Poems about Animals

Most of the poems in this group examine both animal and human traits: typically the animal represents something beyond itself, usually something that ultimately tells us about human nature since, in our anthropomorphic world, animals usually find themselves, in poems as in life, subordinated to humans and in some way reflecting them.

The book contains many other animal poems that might well be compared with those in this group: The Lamb, The Tiger, Aunt Jennifer's Tigers, The Flea, Ode to a Nightingale, Leda and the Swan, The Darkling Thrush, The Windhover.

Emily Dickinson A Narrow Fellow in the Grass (p. 575)

Like a number of the animal poems that follow, this one is ultimately more about people than animals, but the main effect is carefully withheld until the last stanza. The early stanzas seem so pleasant and playful (and so cheerful about the way snakes look and act) that the last stanza is something of a shock in its admission of the speaker's fear. Some things to emphasize: how the mood of playfulness is created in the early stanzas by various scenes that are described without showing any emotional response; how the various suggestions of surprise accumulate into a sense of unpredictability, uncertainty, and finally fear; how the fifth stanza makes a sharp transition by appearing to generalize about the snake as one of "Nature's people" but then abruptly excluding it from the category of things that produce "a transport of cordiality"; how the poem first appears to ignore the traditional human fear of snakes but then at the end draws upon it to ask for the reader's verification; the precision of detail throughout.

Raising the Issue of Authorial Context

This may be a good place to begin to raise the whole issue of authorial context. I like to raise issues like this briefly from time to time. I have had pretty good luck doing this two different ways. (1) Occasionally, when teaching a poem like Dickinson's Narrow Fellow, I assign two or three other poems by the same author, but only talk about them in class very briefly (the "Do you see any similarities" approach in the last few minutes of class). (2) I quietly assign over a period of time several different poems by the same author--one here, one there, with no apparent pattern--but in class make nothing of their connection. Then, when the class has read, say, five or six poems by that particular author, I present them with a ditto sheet containing five or six more poems by that author, and for a day's assignment ask the students to read the new ones, review the ones they've read earlier, and come to class with a list of "characteristics"--things that seem rather distinctively done in that author's work. (Because of copyright laws, one has to use poets who are out of copyright, but there are plenty of good choices represented in the anthology--Shakespeare, Donne, Wordsworth, Herrick, Shelley, and Jonson, for example.) I save this exercise until pretty late in the course, but to do it effectively one must plan for it early and scatter appropriate assignments throughout. I also have a favorite trick in this unit: I throw in one "ringer" poem--an unlabeled poem by someone else which is quite distinctive. So far, every time I have tried this, the problem poem gets isolated in class discussion ("One thing I don't understand," someone says, "is how the poet came to write this one: it's so different from the rest."). Makes for improved confidence, too.

T e x t

3 Speaker

Henry Reed   <u>Lessons</u> <u>of</u> <u>the</u> <u>War:</u> <u>Judging</u> <u>Distances</u> (p.
   406).

My students often argue with each other about
whether there really are two speakers as such in the
poem, or whether, instead, the poem is a reverie in
someone's mind, a reverie in which two voices
recreate a kind of scene. The lack of quotation marks
may contribute to the latter view, but either way of
reading comes to much the same thing. (All dramatic
dialogues are, in one sense, similarly reveries in a
poet's mind.) In any case, it's important to
emphasize the extreme differences of language between
the two voices: the jargon-spouting, thoroughly
"army" drill instructor who dogmatically,
ungrammatically, nonsensically (see especially lines
10-11), and rudely badgers his pupils in lines 1-22
and 31-36; the recruit who rejects the army way for a
highly metaphoric (and perhaps too dreamy and
"poetic") mode of speech which, however, leads him to
common-sense conclusions in lines 25-30 and 37-42.
Some other questions for discussion:
   1. What is accomplished by describing distance
as time in the last line? How does it relate to the
poem's title? Where else in the poem is space
regarded as time?
   2. What passages would you emphasize if you were
considering the poem as (a) an antiwar statement? (b)
an account of military mentality? (c) an analysis of
ways of perceiving natural landscape? (d) a dialogue
between stereotyped articulation and instictive
feeling? (e) a description of man's relationship to
nature? (f) a contrast between things which endure
unchanged and temporal or temporary things? What
passages would you have to omit or de-emphasize in
order to regard the poem in each of these ways? Does
having to ignore part of the poem invalidate the
thesis?

John Betjeman   <u>In</u> <u>Westminster</u> <u>Abbey</u> (p. 407)

The sex of the speaker is indicated here by the
end of the first stanza, and the "lady" is
characterized very quickly, mostly through her own
words and attitudes. Having students detail how she
is characterized and what precisely is implied by

each of her self-righteous, self-centered, and
bigoted statements can be the basis for a good
discussion of how characters characterize themselves
through language. A thorough discussion of
characterization here almost makes a discussion of
"speaker" as such superfluous, for everyone will
recognize that poetry sometimes dramatizes a
character as in a play instead of presenting an
authorical voice speaking directly.

4 Situation and Setting

Robert Browning My Last Duchess (p. 420)

Here there is no commentary at all and no
obvious reflection; this poem is an almost pure
example of a straight dramatic situation. Because it
is spoken by a single character, this kind of poem is
often called a dramatic monologue (see the Glossary).
Characteristic of this kind of poem is a gradual
revelation of the situation and the speaker's
character. The way the speaker gradually gives
himself away, creating a stronger and stronger sense
of horror at his past actions, his present
intentions, and his consistent character creates the
poem's basic effects. Some questions for discussion
or writing assignments:
   1. Describe the dramatic situation. Characterize
the speaker in detail. How is each aspect of his
character suggested? What do the painting and statue
tell you? When do you begin to sense his role in the
earlier events he alludes to? Characterize his "last
duchess." What is the auditor like? How can you tell?
   2. What information is withheld for dramatic
effect? Describe the effects of timing in disclosing
the information. How important is the precise time of
disclosure? Evaluate the structure here against
traditional description of dramatic structure.

W. H. Auden Musee des Beaux Arts (p. 615)

Because of its tight structure and precise,
clean diction, this poem works very well as a basis
for short papers. Two topics have worked especially
well for me:
   1. Look carefully at a copy of the Brueghel
painting, and then write a short essay analyzing
Auden's reading of the painting. What features does
he emphasize? What does he ignore? In what ways does
he narrow the visual focus? Why? Be sure to show how
Auden creates his own effects, how he enforces
artistically his reading of the Brueghel painting.
   2. How does the second stanza of the poem relate
to the generalization of the first stanza? In a short
essay of about 500-600 words, show in detail how
various features of the painting are used to clarify
and make convincing the point Auden makes in stanza
one.

Other things to emphasize in class: the way the people on the ship are characterized, the tones implied in phrases such as "something amazing" or "somewhere to get to," the use of other paintings, the relation of the Icarus myth to the idea of writing a poem about another art form.

John Donne A Valediction: Forbidding Mourning (p. 422)

Because Donne is especially fond of dramatic situations and bold metaphors in all his poems (not just this one), you can create a good exercise on situation and at the same time point ahead to later units on metaphor and authorial context by having students read some other poems by Donne and try to define his distinctive way of visualizing and dramatizing. Other Donne poems in the anthology: The Flea (p. 414), Batter My Heart (p. 349), The Canonization (p. 488), Death Be Not Proud (p. 490).

Poems for Further Study of Situation

Betjeman	In Westminster Abbey (p. 407)
Frost	The Road Not Taken (p. 492)
Hardy	Channel Firing (p. 493)
Jarrell	The Death of the Ball Turret Gunner (p. 439)
Kumin	Woodchucks (p. 383)
Marvell	To His Coy Mistress (p. 512)
Pound	The River-Merchant's Wife: A Letter (p. 362)
Ramsey	The Tally Stick (p. 360)
Roethke	My Papa's Waltz (p. 430)
Snodgrass	Leaving the Motel (p. 379)
Waller	Song (p. 538)
Wayman	Picketing Supermarkets (p. 409)
Wyatt	They Flee from Me (p. 372)

Poems for Further Study of Setting

Coleridge	Kubla Khan (p. 485)
Heaney	Mid-Term Break (p. 407)
Kennedy	In a Prominent Bar in Secaucus One Day (p. 396)
Olds	Leningrad Cemetery, Winter of 1941 (p. 442)
Plath	Black Rook in Rainy Weather (p. 518)
Roethke	My Papa's Waltz (p. 430)

Shelley	Ozymandias (p. 477)
Stevens	Sunday Morning (p. 531)
Thomas	Fern Hill (p. 537)
Wayman	Wayman in Love (p. 365)

A particularly good group to compare might include
some of the following poems, all (like Dover Beach
and Point Shirley) set on beaches or shores:

Hardy	Channel Firing (p. 493)
Keats	On First Looking into Chapman's Homer (p. 508)
Rich	Diving into the Wreck (p. 521)

5 Words

If in earlier classes you have been emphasizing
--from time to time, at least--the significance of
individual words, the focus of this section will be
natural and easy for the class. In my own classes, I
usually teach the poems at the end of this chapter by
asking the students to isolate some key words in the
poems, and we discuss each of these in detail--for
precision of word choice, for the connotations of
each word, for the multiple suggestions (or
"ambiguities") that some words usefully provide, for
allusions to other literature or traditional ideas,
for references to specific facts and events, for the
placement of the word in relation to the larger
emphasis of the poem. Written exercises can be
especially useful in this group; they can be focused
on a single word in a poem or on a group of related
word choices.

Richard Armour Hiding Place (p. 424)

This lovely funny little verse depends on
knowledge of the traditional children's prayer:

> Now I lay me down to sleep,
> I pray the Lord my soul to keep;
> If I should die before I wake,
> I pray the Lord my soul to take.

The main comic effect in Armour's poem depends on
different meanings of the word "keep," making it easy
to illustrate the importance of a single word and
some potentialities of ambiguity.

Robert Herrick Delight in Disorder (p. 428)

A good poem for a paper assignment; one good
topic involves comparison with Jonson's Still to Be
Neat (p. 428). Here are some questions that can be
used to start a discussion or adapted to a paper
assignment:
1. This poem is often regarded as an answer to
Jonson's. What evidence of an answer does the poem
itself bear?
2. What terms associated with disorder have
moral connotations? How does the speaker's stance

toward those connotations differ from the stance of Jonson's speaker? Examine the connotations of each of the following words and describe its effect in the poem: "kindles" (line 2), "thrown" (line 3), "distraction" (line 4), "enthralls" (line 6), "winning" (line 9), "tempestuous" (line 10), "careless" (line 11), "wild" (line 12), "civility" (line 12).

Theodore Roethke   My Papa's Waltz (p. 430)

1. Which details in the poem are disgusting and unpleasant? Which words, phrases, and images suggest more pleasant sensations and feelings? What varieties of emotions does the boy express? How do the connotations of the "waltz" in line 4 relate to those in line 15? to those in the title?
2. Explain the effect of describing the mother's countenance as unable to "unfrown itself" (line 8); of having the ear scrape a buckle (line 12) instead of vice versa.
3. Why is the use of the past tense important?

Gerard Manley Hopkins   Pied Beauty (p. 432)

Which words does Hopkins seem to have invented for this poem? Which other words are used in very unusual senses? How can you be sure of the meaning of words in the first group? What is the specific effect of each word in the second?

Emily Dickinson   After Great Pain (p. 433)

1. Which words and images in the poem help to define "formal" (line 1)? What does "letting go" (line 13) mean? What kinds of release or freedom are involved?
2. How many images or suggestions of stasis or stoppage are there in the poem? How are they spaced? Is there any significance in their spacing and incidence?

William Carlos Williams   The Red Wheelbarrow (p.433)

This is one of the most admired short poems of the twentieth century, and much of its force derives from its careful and precise choice of words and the

way those words are deftly set into place. Your
students may appreciate its art more fully if you ask
them to try to rewrite the poem, keeping exactly the
same visual objects (wheelbarrow, rainwater, and
chickens) but presenting them differently. You can
either set specific rules (change the opening phrase;
keep the objects in the same order, etc.) or give
them a free hand to try to create another poem with
only the same basic materials.

Some questions for discussion: What are the
advantages of a visual scene? What is the function of
the first four words? Why does the poem begin with a
vague term like "so much"? Does the poem's major
effect depend upon an agreement between different
readers on exactly what those words mean? Do the
objects in the poem "stand for" anything? That is,
are they "symbolic"?

Word Order

Defining "normal" word order can be very
difficult, and it may be worth looking back at
several poems you have already taught to see when
word order does not call attention to itself. The
poems in the group here call special attention to
word order, often to create a special emphasis or
meaning, sometimes because of the pressures of meter
or rhyme. The Red Wheelbarrow is one of
those precise, carefully wrought little poems
that are easy to appreciate but very difficult
to discuss; in its choice of simple, evocative
words placed carefully in standard, colloquial
word order, it presents a sharp contrast to
the elaborate word order and manipulation of
most other poems in this group.

Going Backwards

Two or three weeks into the study of poetry--
when a few technical terms have been learned and when
the class has begun to show some real progress in
analytical accomplishment--I like to jump back to a
poem we worked with earlier, sometimes spending ten
or fifteen minutes with it in class or sometimes
asking the class to do papers on it. Either way, I
pick out one aspect of the poem to concentrate on,
giving them a chance to see how much better they can
now handle questions than they could earlier and
allowing them to see how much more fully they can now
experience the poem. The poem London, discussed
briefly in chapter 2 (p. 384), is a particularly good
one to return to, partly because it is so rich and
subtle in tone and partly because its technical
accomplishments are easy to find and worth
emphasizing. Its diction is especially rich
connotatively. Some words worth emphasizing: "mark"
(lines 3, 4); "cry" (lines 5, 6, 9); "ban" (line 7);
"manacles" (line 8); "appalls" (line 10; note its
literal meaning--to make white); "hapless" (line 11);
"blasts" (line 15); "blights" (line 16). Images worth
discussing include the pervasive image of chartering,
the soldier's sigh which "runs in blood" (line 12),
the "marriage hearse" (line 16).

6 Figurative Language

Metaphor can be very hard to teach if one tries to teach individual metaphors in isolation. To many students, individual metaphors often seem mere decoration (sometimes, of course, they are) and therefore rather precious and effete. Good basic metaphors are, of course, more vigorous and functional than that attitude may easily respond to, and I think it is best first to emphasize poems which depend on metaphor, usually a single one or at least a series of related ones. That Time of Year works well as an introduction to metaphor because of its three closely related metaphors for aging and coming death. The first metaphor is expansive and rather general and doesn't give much of a sense of urgency; its focus on a whole season of the year makes the aging process seem long and drawn out, but the other two metaphors are progressively more limited in time, and they project an increasing sense of urgency, as if, by the twelfth line, death were imminent. Because the poem is so carefully structured on the basis of the metaphors (four lines being devoted to each), it is easy for the students to work out and discuss, and with a little prompting from you they will be able to see the progress of the metaphors and their relation to the tone of the poem. Another poem which seems to me to work especially well in a discussion of metaphor is The Death of the Ball Turret Gunner, which has the advantage of being very short and fundamentally based on one metaphor. Its birth metaphor (or rather prebirth metaphor--the gunner is hunched into a fetal position), although not altogether easy to see at first, makes for an especially lively discussion because of the irony of its use in the context of death; the metaphor takes the discussion quickly to the center of the poem. Other poems in the group equally use crucial and interesting metaphors, and it is probably a good idea to offer at least some variety in your selection of poems to discuss in class--some poems that use more submerged metaphors and some that use multiple metaphors as well as those which work from one central one. It may be useful, too, to go back to some poems you have discussed earlier, looking at the function of particular metaphors in the poet's conception of an individual poem.

Questions on the Group

　　1. In which poems is the figurative language
used structurally, to build or unite a particular
section or sections of the poem? When figurative
language is used structurally, how is the transition
made from one section to another? Which poems are
based almost completely on one metaphor?
　　2. Which uses of figurative language in this
group are purely ornamental? In what different ways
does figurative language contribute to meaning? What
other figures besides metaphor are illustrated in the
group?

Poems for Further Study of Figurative Language

Donne   The Canonization (p. 488)
Frost   U.S. 1946 King's X (p. 415)
Mitchell   Woodstock (p. 381)
Piercy   Barbie Doll (p. 378)
Reed   Lessons of the War: Judging Distances
             (p. 406)
Wyatt   They Flee from Me (p. 372)

Metaphor and Simile

Randall Jarrell The Death of the Ball Turret Gunner
　　　(p. 439)

　　The introduction to this group (above) suggests
some things to emphasize. Here is another line of
questioning: What have "sleep" (line 1), "dream"
(line 3), and "nightmare" (line 4) to do with the
basic action of the poem?

John Donne Batter My Heart (p. 439)

　　How appropriate or inappropriate is it to use
sexual metaphors to describe religious experience?
The poet was an Anglican priest: does knowing this
fact make the metaphor seem more appropriate? less
appropriate? more personal? more blasphemous? more
shocking? more decorous?

Symbol

Symbolic poems are often short of detail,
relying on traditional meanings, associations,
and overtones that have accumulated over time.
Sometimes, however, symbolic poems use details
quite explicitly to explore more deeply a
particular (and sometimes neglected) aspect of
a symbol. Which rose poems use details? To
what purpose? In the poems that ignore details
or use them only sparingly, what "meanings" of
rose are most often envoked? How much do you
need to know about roses to read the poems?
Does your knowledge come from real roses, or
literary ones? Compare Waller's <u>Song</u> ("Go,
Lovely Rose!") page 538.

7 Sound and Sight

The Sounds of Poetry

Timing is everything in the poems in this chapter, and you may want to read them aloud yourself or have students practice reading them aloud. In class it can be useful to mark on the board both the placement and the length of pauses; a written exercise on how pauses are indicated and controlled by a poet can be very helpful.

Samuel Taylor Coleridge Metrical Feet (p. 459)

Useful for pointing out the standard English meters.

Arthur W. Monks Twilight's Last Gleaming (p. 459)

As an example of the dactylic meter, very uncommon as a basic meter in English but often used for variation in poems that are basically in another meter. This poem is an example of the so-called double dactyl, a kind of poem very popular with wits in the 1960s.

Anonymous [A Staid Schizophrenic Named Struther], [There Once Was a Pious Young Priest], and [There Once Was a Spinster of Ealing] (p. 460)

Examples of the anapestic meter. Most poems written in anapests tend to be comic, but highly serious--even solemn--poems have been written in anapests.

John Dryden To the Memory of Mr. Oldham (p. 461)

Basically in iambic meter, but with interesting and significant variations--some imitative, some structural, some for emphasis. A good poem to use for a paper assignment on meter.

Donald Justice Counting the Mad (p. 462)

   In what different ways is the echoing of the
nursery rhyme appropriate to the subject matter and
theme of the poem? How does the poem set up a logic
to justify the statements of lines 15-18?

The Way a Poem Looks

e. e. cummings portrait (p. 466)

   1. What accounts for the sense of time having
passed? What evidence is there of contrast between
present and past? How is each viewed by the speaker?
How is the speaker characterized?
   2. Does the poem seem to be mostly about Buffalo
Bill as a person? Buffalo Bill as a performer?
Buffalo Bill as an act? about death? about youth and
vitality? about memory? What parts of the poem would
you emphasize to defend your answer? Are there parts
you would have to ignore?
   3. How does the personification of "Mister
Death" (line 11) differ from the personification in
Donne's Death Be Not Proud (p. 490)? How much of the
difference depends on cummings's withholding of it
until the last line?

Questions on the Group

   1. Poetry was originally oral, and poets and
critics since the seventeenth century have complained
that the printing press is destroying poetry as an
art. In recent years worries have become especially
intense and articulate; some critics insist that
linear form radically distorts sequential experience
by forcing the eyes to translate through a sign
language which is more artificial and less natural
than the aural symbols. Which poems here respond most
directly to that criticism? Which attempt to
coordinate visual and aural effects?
   2. Poems such as Easter Wings obviously rely
upon symbols with thoroughly established meanings and
implications. To what extent does a poem such as
Hollander's You Too? Me Too rely upon established
symbolism? The "beading of Hippocrene" (three-

quarters of the way through You Too? Me Too) and the
"brown shade" (7 lines from the end) are allusions to
Keats's Ode to a Nightingale (p. 506) and Marvell's
The Garden respectively; what does each
contribute to the poem?

   3. Which poems in the group try to imitate
visual experience? Which suggest movement as well as
shape? Do any of the poems try to express temporal
dimensions? Does the visual appearance of any of the
poems actually impede or block one's experience of
meaning? Which of the poems do you think would "hold
up" best upon subsequent readings or viewings? What
are the characteristics which produce such continued
or intensified effects? To what extent are subsequent
readings valid criteria for these works?

   4. The title of John Hollander's poem is a pun.
What other examples are there of puns or visual
comedy?

8 Stanzas and Verse Forms

Many introductory textbooks teach stanza forms by printing a large variety of them and (essentially) asking students to notice their variety and learn their formulas. I have chosen instead to illustrate one form in detail so that students can get to know it well and see not only its basic form but what variations can be played upon it. This way, too, students can begin to see what the form is good for—what can be done within its limits and challenges, and why poets are attracted to a particular form for particular tasks and ideas. The text offers a list of poems that exemplify other stanza forms so that you can do as extensive a unit on them as you like.

William Wordsworth London, 1802 (p. 477)

1. What aspects of English life and institutions are portrayed as stagnant? What evidence does the poem offer? What strategies does the poem use to persuade us that England is stagnant?
2. Why is a poet called on for the solution? Why Milton?

Gwendolyn Brooks First Fight. Then Fiddle (p. 478)

How is the sonnet form appropriate to the poem's theme? Why is the violin an appropriate symbol? Explain the force of "civilize" (line 13).

Elizabethan Sonnets

The sonnets by Sidney, Shakespeare, and Constable survive from a golden age of sonnet writing in the late sixteenth century, an age that set the pattern for expectations of form, subject matter, and tone. The sonnet came to England from Italy via France, and imitations of Petrarch's famous sonnet sequence to Laura became the rage. Thousands upon thousands of sonnets were written in those years, often in sequences of a hundred or more sonnets each;

the sequences usually had a light thread of narrative
which purported to recount a love affair between the
poet and a mistress who was almost always golden-
haired, beautiful, disdainful, and inaccessible. Her
beauty was described in a series of exaggerated
comparisons: her eyes were like the sun, her
teeth like pearls, her cheeks like roses, her
skin like ivory, and so on, but the adherence
to these conventions was always playful, and
it became a game of wit to play variations
upon expectations (My Lady's Presence Makes
the Roses Red. Almost teasing and witty,
these poems were probably not as true to life
as they pretended, but they provided
historically an expectation of what sonnets
were to be.

More Sonnets: A List

Other sonnets in the anthology which might be
used to supplement this unit include:

Browning	How Do I Love Thee (p. 360)
Donne	Batter My Heart (p. 439)
	Death Be Not Proud (p. 490)
Frost	Range-Finding (p. 491)
Keats	On First Looking into Chapman's Homer (p. 508)
Pound	A Virginal (p. 519)
Shakespeare	Let Me Not to the Marriage of True Minds (p. 370)
	Not Marble, Nor the Gilded Monuments (p. 527)
	That Time of Year (p. 435)
Yeats	Leda and the Swan (p. 552)

Sometimes it may be a relief from categories just to assign a particular poem from this section without giving it any labels or suggesting any particular approach to it. Often, too, it is useful to save a week at the end of the course and work on some of the more difficult poems in this section, for example, Sunday Morning. The section can also be mined for additional poems to be taught in individual chapters. I like to reach back here, for example, for the companion Blake poems, The Lamb and The Tiger, when I teach animal poems. And it is also useful as a browsing area for your students to find poems that interest them.

W. H. Auden   In Memory of W. B. Yeats (p. 482)

1. Although a tribute to Yeats, this poem also presents some important ideas about the nature and function of poetry and argues for a particular definition of poetry. What does Auden mean that "poetry makes nothing happen" (line 36)? What evidence does he provide? What does his position imply about verbal communication? about the learning process? about the influence of Yeats's poems? What kinds of results does Auden imply that poems do have? Does Yeats himself seem to have held similar views? (A selection of Yeats's poems appears on pp. 550ff; you may wish to have your students read several of them in connection with Auden's tribute, especially if you plan to discuss different theories of the function and effect of poetry.)

2. The version of the poem printed here is from the Collected Shorter Poems (1966), the only version which is now authorized. Auden's original version of the poem included three additional stanzas, placed between lines 45 and 46 of the version we have been allowed to print. These stanzas claim that time "worships language and forgives" all kinds of human weaknesses in those "by whom it lives." The two examples cited are Rudyard Kipling and Paul Claudel. For what might Kipling and Claudel need to be forgiven? How does the attitude expressed toward Claudel and Kipling relate to ideas about the effects of poetry expressed elsewhere in the poem? In introducing the 1966 edition, Auden defended his revision of several poems, saying that he had never "consciously at any rate" tried to revise "former thoughts and feelings" but had felt free to change

the language in which he expressed them. Does Auden's account adequately explain the revision in this poem? What other possible reasons might there be for revision? Might there be decent and respectable reasons for a writer to mislead readers about revisions and changes of mind?

William Blake   The Lamb (p. 483)
William Blake   The Tiger (p. 484)

Blake seems to have intended these as companion poems. The Lamb is from Songs of Innocence, The Tiger from Songs of Experience; often a poem from the former volume has a companion poem which emphasizes a fiercer, darker, less innocent side of life. Comparing the two poems makes for a lively discussion (or a good paper topic); notice how the poems qualify each other's effect when read side by side. Some things to discuss and emphasize: internal evidence that the poems should be read as a pair, the use of repetition, the emphasis upon each animal as an appropriate symbol of creation, the ways the two animals seem opposite, the ways they seem identical, the devices used to make them seem both at the same time. You might wish to note, too, how The Lamb makes use of both the pastoral tradition and of Christian metaphors from the New Testament, and how, in The Tiger, the alteration of only one word indicates the changes in perspective that have been rendered between the first and last stanzas.

Samuel Taylor Coleridge   Kubla Khan (p. 485)

List all the visual details in the poem. Which visual effects depend upon the surprising juxtaposition of things not normally seen together? How do the poem's "sound effects" (rhythm, rhyme, onomatopoeic words, etc.) relate to the visual effects?

e. e. cummings   chanson innocente (p. 486)

Explain the logic and effect of "eddieandbill" (line 6) and "bettyandisbel" (line 14). Explain the force of "mud-luscious" (lines 2-3) and "puddle-wonderful" (line 10). How does the interaction of the children and the old man relate to the tension between new life and tradition? Explain the implication of the allusion to Pan.

Emily Dickinson

   Many of the Dickinson poems printed in this
section are not usually anthologized, and these
poems suggest a poet more playful, more comic, more
fanciful and more flirtatious than the somewhat
somber Emily Dickinson that emerges from some of the
more familiar lyrics. Dickinson--as represented in
this book--is a good poet to study in combination
with Adrienne Rich, not only because Rich remembers
and consciously departs from her mode of seeing and
telling, but also because Dickinson's quiet
but resolute bursting of formal bonds
resembles so closely the Rich of an early poem
like Aunt Jennifer's Tigers (p. 572).

Emily Dickinson   Because I Could Not Stop for Death
      (p. 487)

   1. How do you respond to the fantasy of the
journey? What details of the journey seem the most
significant? Are they most significant because of
their allegorical meaning? because of their visual
force? because their everyday simplicity makes death
seem friendly and natural rather than remote and
dreadful?
   2. Are you bothered by the speaker's claim to
have been dead for "Centuries" (line 21)? why or why
not? What is implied by the speaker's inability to
stop for death (line 1)?

John Donne   The Canonization (p. 488)

   Characterize the person to whom the poem seems
to be addressed. What lines in the poem seem to
answer specifically objections raised by that person?
Explain the canonization metaphor fully and show how
the structure of the poem depends upon it.

John Donne   Death Be Not Proud (p. 490)

   1. What is gained by personalizing Death? by
personifying it? Describe the effect of the direct
address in lines 1-2. What is your tone of voice when
you read "poor Death" (line 4)?
   2. Summarize each step in the argument which
"proves" Death not to be very powerful. Which part of
the argument seems to you most effective? Why? How
much is your judgement of effectiveness conditioned
by your own ideas of death and immmortality? How many

times are sleep and death compared? What is the point
of each comparison?
   3. Describe the speaker's final claims: Are they
confident? boastful? smug? proud? In what sense are
the claims justified by what has happened in the
poem? In what sense are they not justified?

Robert Frost   Range-Finding (p. 491)

   This poem is easy to misread, and students who
think of Frost as a nature poet sometimes respond so
strongly to the human violation of nature in the
first part of the poem that they miss the later
emphasis on victimization and killing within nature
itself. The poem divides neatly as an Italian sonnet
(defined in the Glossary), and some emphasis on the
poem's form can clarify how crisply the argument is
set up (as well as prepare for later, more detailed
discussion of verse forms). Things to discuss: the
details that provoke sympathy for injured nature in
the first 8 lines, the details that suggest nature's
resilience, the contrasting descriptions of the web
in lines 1 and 9-11, the characterization of the
spider, the randomness of human destruction versus
the spider's calculated, natural preying. A good poem
for a paper assignment; you can direct the students
toward an analysis of how the poem's form and
structure relate to its depiction of human and
natural preying.

Thomas Hardy   The Darkling Thrush (p. 494)

   The thrush clearly stands for something in the
speaker's mind, and an introduction to issues of
symbolism can be accomplished through the poem.
Mainly, of course, the poem is about the "Century's
corpses" (line 10), and it is useful to have students
enumerate all the indications of death and ending in
the first part of the poem, so that the unexplained
cheerfulness of the thrush has a human context to
operate against. Some teachers like to raise the
issue of whether the century really ends in 1900 or
1899. It's good for 10 or 15 minutes of lively and
often heated discussion, but I'm not sure it has
anything to do with the poem; besides, Hardy is
right: centuries start with 1 and end with 00.

Gerard Manley Hopkins   The Windhover (p. 498)

The invented words and unusual rhythm (Hopkins called it "sprung rhythm": see the Glossary) are likely to dominate any discussion of this poem, but if you are teaching it as an animal poem you may also wish to emphasize the appropriateness of the bird as a religious symbol and what features of the bird Hopkins emphasizes in making it symbolic.

A. E. Housman   To an Athlete Dying Young (p. 500)

1. What is "the road all runners come" (line 5)? How much resonance does the metaphor take from the idea of life as a journey? Does it make any difference that this kind of metaphor (road of life, life as sojourn or pilgrimage, etc.) is common in ordinary conversation, in literature, and in religious tradition?
2. Which important words from stanza 3 recur in the last stanza? What is the purpose of the repetition? How does the handling of time in the last stanza allow a different emphasis?
3. How do you respond to the stanza beginning "Smart lad"? How much force has the long argument that the athlete is lucky not to have lived to experience the humiliation of age? How much of your response depends on certain ideas you bring to the poem: ideas about death? about recognition of one's accomplishments? about pomp and pageantry? about time?

Ben Jonson   Epitaph on Elizabeth, L. H. (p. 504)

It was customary to abbreviate titles and last names on tombstones in Jonson's time, and it has been suggested that Elizabeth was titled (L = Lady), a small child, and the last in her family line (see line 10). In any case, Jonson uses the epitaph as a metaphor for talking about poetry and the demands of the epigram in particular. Some questions for discussion:
1. What details suggest the poem's self-consciousness about the tradition of the epigram? What dramatic situation is implied by "Reader, stay" (line 2)? What different meanings are implied in "a little" (line 2)?
2. Is line 4 simply a courtly compliment or does it make a serious philosophical statement? line 6? How can you tell in each case? What attitudes does the poem take toward death? toward the ongoing world? toward the life of noblesse oblige?

3. Is the poem witty? Is it funny? Does it contain a "sting"? Describe the poem's tone.

Ezra Pound In a Station of the Metro (p. 519)

1. Explain as precisely as possible the relationship between the first and second lines. Is the transition visual? associational? intellectual? emotional? What is your precise feeling about each object you are asked to consider or feel. Explain the force of the word "apparition" (line 1).
2. Pound was, early in the twentieth century, one of the leading exponents of "imagism," a movement which emphasized (among other things) the use of precisely defined and concentrated images to create a unified impression. Detail the ways in which the poem satisfies imagism's aims.

Ezra Pound A Virginal (p. 519)

1. To whom are lines 1 and 9 addressed? What qualities ascribed to "her" (line 1) account for the speaker's single-mindedness? Does the poem dramatize her physical attractiveness? her values? What is the present state of the relationship? How much precise detail is given about the relationship? By what means are we led to infer more than we are told?
2. Why does the poem use exaggerated statements such as that about the "lightness" of "surrounding air" (line 3)? How effective are such statements? Which senses do they appeal to? Why is the sheath metaphor (lines 2,8) appropriate?
3. Does the poem generalize about masculine traits and habits? about feminine ones? Compare A Virginal to They Flee from Me (p. 553); which poem seems more personal? more universal? Are "personal" and "universal" necessarily opposites?
4. Does the title at first mislead you? What kind of metaphor does the title imply? Describe the full implications of the title.

Edwin Arlington Robinson Richard Cory (p. 524)

What substitutes for time as organizing devices in the poem? How much detail about Richard Cory do we actually get? How many of the details are really only general impressions? What kinds of effects are produced by this cumulative method of organizing the poem? How does the method of presenting details relate to the poem's surprise ending?

Stephen Spender An Elementary School Classroom in a
    Slum (p. 529)

    Some questions for discussion: Who or what is the villain of the poem? How are negative feelings aroused? Toward whom and what are positive responses aroused? How? What different things do the maps represent to the children? to the speaker? Why are colors not mentioned until the last four lines?

Wallace Stevens <u>Sunday Morning</u> (p. 531)

1. Describe the situation and setting of the poem in detail. Why is the opening description so elegant and colorful? What different activities and attitudes traditionally associated with Sunday morning set up the expectations which the poem exploits? How is each expectation used?

2. When the poem was first published, an editor persuaded Stevens to omit stanzas 2, 3, and 6. Stevens insisted that the remaining stanzas be printed in the following order: 1, 8, 4, 5, 7--because (he said) "the order is necessary to the idea." Try reading the poem in that form and compare the effect. Which omissions seem the most important to the shorter version? Why? Why do you think Stevens insisted on changing the order in the shorter version?

Dylan Thomas <u>Do</u> <u>Not</u> <u>Go</u> <u>Gentle</u> <u>into</u> <u>That</u> <u>Good</u> <u>Night</u> (p. 536)

The powerful effects of repetition are easily visible here, and you might want to spend a few minutes noticing how the rich rhyme and the repetition of whole lines add both to the compactness of statement in the poem and to the soothing effects of ritual. This is a good place, too, to put in a word for the uses of rhyme--and possibly for fixed poetic forms, if you plan later to spend a bit of time on verse forms. <u>Do</u> <u>Not</u> <u>Go</u> <u>Gentle</u> is a villanelle.

Dylan Thomas <u>Fern</u> <u>Hill</u> (p. 537)

Compare it to Lawrence's <u>Piano</u> (p. 555). Each poem centers on a physical object as the vehicle to consider the past. How do the treatments of the object differ? How do different poetic intentions account for the different treatments? How much of the difference is due to the object chosen. In what ways are the poems similar?

Dylan Thomas <u>In</u> <u>My</u> <u>Craft</u> <u>or</u> <u>Sullen</u> <u>Art</u> (p. 538)

Compare the image of "spindrift" pages (line 14) with Shakespeare's presentation of a poem's lastingness in <u>Not</u> <u>Marble,</u> <u>Nor</u> <u>the</u> <u>Gilded</u> <u>Monuments</u> (p. 527). How literal in each is the poet's definition of his aims? of his audience?

Walt Whitman   When Lilacs Last in the Dooryard
     Bloomed (p. 539)

    1. How important is chronology to the
organization of the poem? What varieties of
repetition help to unite the poem?
    2. Try moving some of the sections around;
describe the difference in effect produced by the
different sequence. What principles seem to underlie
the patterns of sectioning? How do the structural
problems of longer poems differ from those in short
poems?

Richard Wilbur   The Beautiful Changes (p. 545)

    1. Which words in stanza 1 emphasize the visual
similarity between landscape and seascape? Explain
the two transformations that are compared in lines 4-
6.
    2. Which words and phrases depend upon the
poet's close visual observation? Which ones ask you
to revise a habitual way of seeing or thinking about
common things?
    3. Detail each of the "changes" the poem
describes. How does each relate to the one before and
after it? What, according to the poem, is the
ultimate change?
    4. On pp. 448ff is a series of poems which use
roses as a symbol of beauty's shortness and
fragility. How does the use of roses in stanza three
differ from that traditional usage? What indications
are there in the poem that the poet is consciously
manipulating the rose symbol? What other
manipulations of expectations are there in the poem?
What effect is produced by the repeated assertion
that beauty changes?

POEMS BY BLACK POETS: A LIST

Poems by black poets are placed in appropriate groups throughout the book rather than being set off in a separate section; because they are not so labeled and because they are not all about blackness itself, students may not realize which of the poems collected in this book are by blacks. You may wish to create a special group or series of subgroups involving some of the following black poets:

Maya Angelou	Africa (p. 479)
Gwendolyn Brooks	First Fight. Then Fiddle (p. 478)
Michael Harper	Dear John, Dear Coltrane (p. 464)
Robert Hayden	Those Winter Sundays (p. 374)
	Frederick Douglass (p. 496)
Langston Hughes	Harlem (A Dream Deferred) (p. 501)
	The Negro Speaks of Rivers (p. 502)
	Theme for English B (p. 502)
Etheridge Knight	Hard Rock Returns to Prison (p. 383)
Audre Lorde	Recreation (p. 369)
Gabriel Okara	Piano and Drums (p. 515)
Dudley Randall	Ballad of Birmingham (p. 520)

APPENDIX: A SAMPLE ANALYSIS OF <u>TO</u> <u>HIS</u> <u>COY</u> <u>MISTRESS</u>

The title suggests the situation--a man is speaking to his beloved--and before we are far into the poem we recognize his familiar argument: let's not wait, let's make love now. But much more is going on in the poem than this simple "message."

Seduction is a promising subject, but it is nearly as easy to be dull on this subject as on less fascinating ones, and the subject has inspired some very dreary poetry. The interest and power of this poem depend on more than the choice of subject, however useful that subject is in whetting a reader's expectations. No reader is likely to use the poem as a handbook for his own life, and few readers are likely to read it at a moment when their own lives parallel precisely the poem's situation. Its relevance is of a larger kind: it portrays vividly and forcefully a recognizable situation, saying something <u>about</u> that situation but (more important) making us react to the situation and feel something about it. Experiencing a poem involves not only knowing what it says but also feeling the pleasures provided by its clever management of our own ideas and emotions. All poems have a design on us--they try to make us feel certain things--and the full experience of a poem requires full recognition of the complexities of design so that we can feel specific emotions and pleasures--not only the general ones of contemplating seduction.

Let's begin at the beginning. What do you expect of a poem about a would-be seduction? One thing you can be almost certain of is that it will contain attractive images of physical enjoyment. The first verse-paragraph (lines 1-20) contains such images, and so does the third (especially lines 33-38). The first set of images suggest the languorous, lazy appeal of a timeless world where physical enjoyment seems to fill all time and all space. First are images of rich sensuousness; the leisurely contemplation of enjoyment, the timeless walks in exotic lands, the finding of precious stones, the luxury of delaying the supreme moment. Gradually sensuousness becomes sensuality, and the speaker imagines himself praising various parts of the girl's body. In line 33, the poem returns to sexual contemplation but with much more intensity. Now the girl seems to be not only a passive object of admiration but a live, breathing, perspiring, passionate respondent. And a moment later, the speaker projects the beauty and energy of the love act itself. He suggests something of his anticipation of supreme ecstasy by the vividness and intensity of the images and language he uses: from the languid, flowing, floating suggestions of the early lines through the breathless anticipation of lines 33-37 to the violence of lines 41-44 with their explicit visualization of the union, the rolling into one, of "strength" and "sweetness."

But not all the poem portrays glorious pleasure. The second verse paragraph (lines 21-32) contains some pretty grim stuff. Instead of the endless languor of unhurried walks and exotic places in the early lines, we have anxiety and consciousness of time--a hurrying chariot, moving up fast from behind. And instead of the centuries of body-worship, eternity consists of vast deserts. Grimmest of all is the image of a different kind of fall than the one the speaker desires; the carefully preserved virginity of the girl, the speaker imagines, will be tested and destroyed in the grave by worms. The speaker summarizes with gross understatement and macabre humor in lines 31-32:

> The grave's a fine and private place,
> But none, I think, do there embrace.

The contrast of all that grimness of future dryness and death emphasizes (first) the unreal romanticism of the timeless world which, according to the speaker, the girl seems to want, and (second) the vividly portrayed sensual pleasures of a potential moment right now. Such contrasts work for us as well as for the presumed girl; in fact, they are part of a carefully contrived argument that organizes the poem. We might well have expected, just from the title and the opening lines, that the poem would be organized as a formal argument. The first words of each paragraph clearly show the outlines: (1) "Had we . . ." (If we had no limits of time or space); (2) "But . . ." (But we do have such limits); (3) "Now, therefore." The poem is cast as a long, detailed hypothetical syllogism; it uses the form of a standard argument, with vivid examples and carefully contrived rhetoric, to suggest the urgency of enjoying the moment. It is a specious argument, of course, but real people have fallen for worse ones. But this isn't "real life"; the story doesn't even end. As in most other poems (and unlike most drama and fiction), the "plot" and its resolution have little to do with the final effect. Part of the point here is to notice the flaw in the argument. A good logician could show you that the speaker commits the fallacy of the "denied antecedent," that is, he proves what cannot happen but fails to prove what can. Seduction seldom, of course, gets worked out in purely logical terms, and so in one sense the logic of the argument doesn't matter—any more than whether the speaker finally seduces the girl. But in another sense it matters a great deal and contributes to our complex experience of the poem. For if we spot the illogic and find it amusing (since the argument is obviously an effective one, logical or not), we not only feel the accuracy of the poem's observation about seduction but we experience something important about the way words work. Often their effect is more far-reaching than what they say on a literal level, just as this poem reaches much further than any literal statement of its "message" or "meaning." Poetry often exploits the fact that words work in such mysterious ways; in fact, most poems, in one way or another, are concerned with the fact that words may be used suggestively to open out on horizons beyond logical and syntactical categories.

Reading a poem about seduction is hardly the same thing as getting seduced, and only a very peculiar poet or reader would expect it to be, though some of the censorship controversies over the teaching of poems like this may sometimes imply that life and art are the same thing. Anyone who thinks they are is bound to be disappointed by a poem about seduction, or about anything else. One does not go to a poem instead of being seduced, or as a sublimation, or as a guide. A poem about anything does not intend to be the thing itself, or even to recreate it precisely. Poetry, like other literature, is an ordered imitation of <u>perceived</u> reality expressed in words. By definition, by intention, and by practice, poetry modifies life to its own artistic ends, "ordering"—that is, making meaningful—what is only a version in any case. What poetry offers us is not life itself, naked and available, but a perspective (perceived reality) on some recognizable situations or ideas; not Truth with a capital T, but interpretations and stances: not passion itself, but words that evoke associations and memories and feelings. A poem can provide an angle of vision which in "real life" is often blurred through our closeness to experience. And just as the poet fictionalizes—whether he begins with a real event or not—we as readers end with his version, which exists in tension with other things we know, about words, about poetry, about arguments, about seduction, about everything. That tension tests not the "truth" of the poet's vision but the effects produced by the poem; the more we know, the richer these effects are likely to be.

Anyone with developed sensitivities and a modest amount of knowledge of the suggestiveness of words can find the crucial words that express and evoke the sensual appeal. The devices of contrast (the flowing Ganges flanked by rubies vs. vast deserts; the spacious wandering vs. the confinement of a marble vault; eternal adoration vs. those traditional symbols of mortality ashes and dust) may be readily seen by anyone willing to look at the poem carefully. In short, much of the poem is readily available to almost any reader who looks carefully; much of its power is right there on the page, and a reader need make only a minimal effort to experience it.

But a number of things in the poem require a special skill or knowledge. The poem's parody of a hypothetical syllogism is only available to those who can recognize a hypothetical syllogism and see the distortion in this one. Of course, not recognizing the syllogism is not too serious, as long as the reader "senses" the falsity of the argument and finds the incongruity in its effectiveness; he simply misses a joke which is part of the poem's complexity. But some other matters in the poem are more crucial for lack of knowedge about them would not only drain the poem of some of its richness but might even force a misunderstanding of what the poem says on its most literal level.

Look, for instance, at the following words: "coy" (title) and "coyness" (line 2); "mistress" (title); "complain" (line 7); "vegetable" (line 11); "adore" (line 15). All of these words are common enough, but each offers a problem in interpretation because of changes in meaning. The poem was written more than three hundred years ago, in the mid-17th century, and many words used in a specific way then have changed over the years. Words are, in a sense, alive and everchanging; change is a part of the excitement of language as well as a potential frustration, and if we construe each of these words exactly as it is construed now we will be badly misled. The most obvious change in meaning is in the word "mistress," for to us it implies a specific sexual relationship, one that would make the elaborate seduction plea here seem a little late. The most common 17th-century meaning of "mistress" was simply "a woman who has command over a man's heart; a woman who is loved and courted by a man; a sweetheart, lady-love." This definition comes from the <u>Oxford</u> <u>English</u> <u>Dictionary</u>, a valuable reference

guide that lists historical as well as modern
meanings, with detailed examples of usages. The OED
can also show us that the new meaning of "mistress"
was coming into use when this poem was written, and
perhaps the meanings are played off against each
other, as a kind of false lead; such false leads are
common in poetry, for poets often like to toy with
our expectations and surprise us.

"Coy" and "coyness" offer a similar problem; in
modern usage they usually suggest playful teasing,
affectation, coquettishness. But originally they
suggested shyness, modesty, reluctance, reserve, not
simply the affectation of those things. Of course, we
find out very little about the girl herself in this
poem (except what we can infer from the things the
speaker says to her and the way he says them), but we
are not led to think of her as sly and affected in
her hesitancy to receive her lover's advances.

"Complain" and "adore" are more technical. The
former indicates a lover going through the ritual of
composing a "complaint"—a poem which bewails his
misery because of a lady's disdain. Thus, the speaker
here self-deprecatingly (but comically) imagines
himself (in the unreal, timeless world of the first
verse paragraph) as a pining swain, while his love is
luxuriating half across the earth, oblivious to his
pain. Obviously, the speaker wants no part of such
sado-masochistic romantic nonsense; he prefers sexual
pleasure to poetic posing. "Adore" technically means
to worship as a deity; there is a certain irony in
regarding the girl's body as an object of religious
worship, but this speaker carries through his version
of the girl's fantasy, modestly refusing to name
those parts he wishes to devote thirty thousand years
to, and regarding her "heart" (usually synonymous
with soul in the Renaissance) as the ultimate
conquest for the last age.

The term "vegetable" is even more complex, for
it depends on a whole set of physiological/
psychological doctrines in the Renaissance. According
to those doctrines, the human soul was made up of
three souls which corresponded to the different
levels of living matter. The Vegetable Soul man
possessed in common with plants and animals; the
Sensible Soul he possessed in common with animals;
the Rational Soul was possessed by man alone. The
Vegetable Soul was the lowest and had only the powers
of reproduction, nourishment, and growth. The sense,
the passions, and the imagination were under the
power of the Sensible Soul. A "vegetable love" would
be without feeling or passion, appropriate to the
lowest form of life. The speaker thus reduces the
notion of timeless, romantic nonphysical love to what

he considers its proper level--a subhuman, absurd
one. He pictures love without physical involvement
not as a higher spiritual attraction but rather as a
lower, nonsentient one.

Several other parts of the poem similarly
require historical knowledge. Lines 33-36 depend upon
Renaissance love psychology which considered
physiological reactions (the rosy skin, perspiration)
to be stimulated by the release of "animal spirits"
in the blood. This release happened when the emotions
were heightened by sight of the beloved; phantasms
from the eye descended to the soul and released the
animal spirits. The soul was thus "present" in the
physiological response (the animal spirits), and the
speaker pictures it here as involved in the very
moment of desire, trying to unite--through the body--
with the soul of the beloved. This love psychology
may seem somewhat naive, but it is a humbling
experience to try to explain our modern notions of
how eyes and emotions relate to bodily processes.

The final two lines of the poem depend heavily
upon specific knowledge. First there is an allusion
to Greek mythology--an allusion which actually began
several lines before the end with the reference to
Time's slow-chapped (i.e., slow-jawed) power.
According to the myth, Chronos (Time) ate all his
children except Zeus (who had been hidden by Rhea),
and Zeus afterward seized Chronos' power as chief of
the gods. Zeus later made the sun stand still to
lengthen his love night with Alcmene. We cannot, the
speaker says, make time stand still as Zeus did, but
we can speed it up. His argument assumes the 17th-
century belief that each sex act made a person's life
one day shorter. The speaker keeps insisting that the
coming of death--time's end--is easier to cope with
if you have something interesting to do while you
wait.

Up to now we have not even mentioned the man who
wrote the poem, Andrew Marvell. Whether Marvell ever
had such a coy friend as this poem implies is not
very important to us (though it may have been very
important to him). For us, the relevant point is the
fiction of the poem--regardless of whether that
fiction is based on actual fact. But some facts about
authorship may be very useful to us as readers of the
poem, as long as we use them to help us with the poem
and do not simply engage in biographical speculation.
In many cases, knowledge about the author is likely
to help us recognize the poet's distinctive
strategies, and reading other poems by him often
reveals his attitudes or devices so that we can read
any one poem with more clarity, security, and
depth.

A reader may experience a poem in a satisfactory way without all of the special knowledge I have been describing, but additional knowledge and developed skill can heighten the experience of almost any poem. Poems do not "hide" their meaning, and good poets usually communicate rather quickly in some basic way. Rereadings, reconsiderations, and the application of additional knowledge allow us to hear resonances built into the poem, qualities that make it enjoyable to experience again and again. We have really only begun to look closely at this particular poem, and if you were to continue to reread it carefully, you would very likely discover richnesses which this brief discussion has not even suggested. The route to meaning is often clear on first reading a poem, but the full possibilities of experience may require more time, energy, and knowledge of the right questions to ask.

DRAMA

TEACHING DRAMA

Many teachers find plays harder to teach than either stories or poems, perhaps because they are usually longer, sometimes more complex structurally, and always seem slightly out of place on a page instead of the stage. But these difficulties can be turned into virtues, for the features they represent all need to be discussed openly in class, and the last of them (page/stage) will almost inevitably dominate the classroom time you have to spend on any play. Your students will almost certainly need guidance and attention on issues of production and staging, and probably will get involved rather more quickly in this kind of discussion than they do on more literary issues. Even students with no experience in play production--or even in seeing plays--often become fascinated with questions of how words and actions are fleshed out on the stage. As the discussions in the opening chapters suggest, it is often a good idea to begin with various staging questions when you begin to teach any play.

The age-old custom of reading aloud in class, if not done too often (boredom, predictability, embarrassment) or with too high expectations of how students will do at first (fear of failure, lack of confidence) can be especially effective in teaching plays. Usually it's best to do short scenes only; interrupt to ask questions about movement, or gesture, or intonation and (later) of interpretation. Change parts often so that everyone gets involved. Diagrams on the board can help chart space and movement. Walk-throughs may be too discouraging at first (students will unconsciously, or perhaps consciously, compare each other and themselves to actors on film or TV); keep them conscious of how it ought to look and feel to an audience. Help them see how little things--a little shift in tone, a slight movement--make all the difference. The fact that your students have grown up on television and with movies is a terrific asset in teaching drama, and gradually you can show them artistic differences between modes by getting them to notice how the conventions of a stage are quite different from the "realism" of a camera that can go (almost) anywhere. Participation can be a great asset in the drama part of your course. But beware of the class ham. You may have to alter your strategy if there is a too experienced actor who knows it all, or a class clown, or a born disrupter who takes advantage of the temptations of theatricality.

The discussions that follow suggest, in most cases, some things to emphasize that do not come up for much attention in the chapters themselves. Often we suggest ways to point to issues in later chapters, or to reemphasize in plays further along things that have come up earlier. Nothing is so boring to students as the rigidity of teaching one work as exclusively one thing--character, for example--and another as exclusively something else. We hope that the discussion will suggest to you some ways of varying, and complicating, the main emphases in the chapters. For most of the plays, we have also included questions to stimulate discussion or to serve as a basis for paper topics.

1 EXPERIENCING DRAMA

Harold Pinter   The Black and White (p. 558)

Unless they have been involved in dramatic productions in high school, students usually have little knowledge of staging, stage business, or the importance of physical gestures. The Black and White, because of its brevity and simplicity, offers a good opportunity to look at the importance to dramatic effect of small gestures. A good way to introduce staging issues is to ask students to do a brief written exercise before class, or ask them to spend the first ten minutes of class writing a paragraph-- with the text in front of them--on how they would dress one of the women and what facial expressions they would ask her to assume. One way to set up the discussion is to divide the class in half and have some write about one woman, some about the other, and then compare their decisions. The crucial question to get to in class involves how dress, facial expressions, voice inflections, and gestures contribute to--in fact, are--the dramatic center of this play. If you use this strategy, have some students read their papers in class and ask them to defend their decisions by pointing to lines in the text. Get them to notice how the women repeat each other's phrases and how similar they are in age, in habits, even in their idiosyncrasies. Ask them to suggest how they would make the clothes and gestures of each reflect the other character without having them be identical. And why not identical?

A second alternative, which could be turned into a paper assignment of three or four pages, or into a class discussion of 20-30 minutes, involves blocking out the stage action. How would the blocking differ if you were doing the sketch as a film? Would you use "extras" in either case as a backdrop for the interaction between the two women? How important is timing in the conversation? How long would it take to play the scene appropriately? Where would the key pauses be? What would each woman's "body language" be like? How old do you imagine the women to be? What evidence does the play present about the previous meetings between the women? about their habits more generally? How important is the lighting? How much color would you include in the clothing, props, and background? Why?

Anton Chekhov   The Brute (p. 566)

The Brute also presents good opportunities to
discuss various aspects of theatrical production in a
relatively short and simplified form. Again, a brief
written assignment may be useful for setting up the
discussion, and again, an analysis of character is a
good way to make the transition to visual, audial,
and staging effects. Chekhov's description of both
Mrs. Popov and Smirnov is very brief; have your
students describe each character more fully,
detailing the way both would present themselves at
first appearance. Some questions of definition: How
would you have Mrs. Popov betray her ritualistic
fondness of grief? What clothes, gestures, or facial
expressions might provide a contrast to her gloomy
words? How subtle does the contrast need to be to
make the play work theatrically?
    Again, dividing the class into groups or teams
may be a way of highlighting the issues, but I
suggest that for The Brute you do the division
somewhat differently. Have one group responsible for
stage props, another for costumes, a third for
blocking and stage movement, a fourth for the
gestures and intonation of actors, and work on a
short scene together. The discussion can't go far
before the students will readily see how intertwined
the questions are and how someone will have to
provide clear direction based on a certain
interpretation of the play.

2 STRUCTURE AND STAGE

Anonymous   The Sacrifice of Isaac (p. 583)

Below I will be offering critical and
pedagogical discussion, questions, and suggestions
that may be of some help to you in talking about The
Sacrifice of Isaac in class, but I cannot do it that
way myself. The Abraham-Isaac episode in Bible or
play causes me great difficulty. I feel like Ivan
Karamazov. Can a beneficent, all-powerful God test
one of his people so cruelly? Well, of course God
knows all along that he will not let Abraham kill his
son. But what kind of God is this who can so play on
a father's feelings? In my narrow and benighted view
it's only if Abraham had refused would my kind of god
have honored him. No, this story disturbed me even
before I was a father. I don't know whether you can
begin with such troubled questions, but I do and get
to the play somewhat later.
    I translate the theme sometimes from the
religious to other spheres too. Is it worth
sacrificing a generation to create a more perfect
state or society? Could you in cold blood kill a
friend if you thought (or knew) it would save two,
three, five, a dozen others? Under what circumstances
is it justifiable to take a life (not by having the
state or a professional do it, but by your own hand)?
To what extent is it immoral to benefit from acts of
violence that others do but you would not do for
yourself? Are you a vegetarian? Would you kill a
fish? a chicken? a steer? a hog? Is there any
comparison between the religious play The Sacrifice
of Isaac and the mundane story Boys and Girls by
Alice Munro?
    Isaac is one of the many plays in this volume
treating parents and children. Some of you may want
to stress this aspect right away, pick up Hamlet in
this chapter, Hedda in the next, and go right on
through Death of a Salesman to Oedipus.

    The Biblical story of Abraham centers on the
desire of that patriarch for a son to carry his
lineage and to beget the nations that God had
promised would follow him, and it emphasizes the
miracle of Isaac's birth. Although these matters are
mentioned, they are not emphasized as they might have
been in a more purely theological play; instead, the
play focuses on the relation between father and son

in terms of mutual affection, trust, and consolation.

The play shows solid craftsmanship: the fact that the Mother does not appear, for example: had Sarah appeared, strong dramatic effects, such as the counterpointing of the audience's knowledge of Isaac's destiny with her farewell, believing that he will return, would have been introduced and would have distracted from the main thrust of the action.

Using the relation between father and son as example, the play presents the conflict between principle (here that obedience to God is the first duty of man) and the emotions and needs of individuals in specific situations. Even the learned man who comments at the end does not spin theological abstractions about the analogy between God-Jesus and Abraham-Isaac. Rather he speaks to men and women in an age of high infant and child mortality rates to comfort them.

The theme of the play is announced in Abraham's speech in lines 13-15, "I love no thing so much, y-wis, / Except thine own self, dear Father of bliss, / As Isaac here, my own sweet son." Abraham is narrowly saved from hubris by the parenthetical expression of his primary love for God. His syntax suggests that he is a character with two strong loyalties, ready to be tested. The brief appearance of Isaac at the end of the prayer further presents the strength of his love for his son. Later when Abraham prays to know what kind of animal to sacrifice, the dramatic thrust is strengthened. He has acted without consideration of the possible answers, as Oedipus did when he swore to punish the murderer of Laius.

The central and dramatic part of the play is the journey of Abraham and Isaac to the mountain of sacrifice, their arrival, and their preparations. At first the struggle of Abraham is expressed in four brief asides; outwardly he is calm and strong. Isaac, at first all obedience and affection, becomes curious and by line 154 has discovered the truth. Now the struggle between Abraham the servant of God and Abraham the loving father can be expressed directly in the dialogue with Isaac. Isaac's responses vary rapidly, and the details of each are chosen to heighten Abraham's struggle and increase the pathos of the scene—his complaint in lines 192-93, his attempt to comfort his father, his desire to spare his mother, his request for a blessing, and his prayer for a blindfold and a swift death. The constant alternation of strong emotions moves the play forward rapidly though there is little physical action. In the fifth and sixth asides and his final speech before the appearance of the Angel, for example, Abraham moves from decision to indecision and back. After the climax the dramatic thrust is preserved by the contrast between Abraham's joy and relief and Isaac's shifting moods--apprehension, joy, then apprehension again as in lines 377-78, "But, father, will I stoop down low, / Ye will not kill me with your sword, I trow?" Even after the appearance of God, Isaac's joy changes to apprehension when he says that he will never return to this mountain.

The contrast between the consistent though divided emotions of the mature man and the volatility of the child give further power to this picture of the relation between parent and child.

Questions for Classroom Use

Plot

1. Abraham's first speech takes the form of a prayer. What does the author manage to convey in this prayer? How do the audience's prior notions about Abraham affect the necessity for an extensive exposition?

2. How might we consider lines 13-15 as initiating the real action of the play?

3. Why is the character of Isaac introduced briefly at the end of this first section of the play?

4. What form does the complicating action of the play take?

5. What is Abraham's immediate reaction to the command of the angel? How does the author establish a dialectic between Abraham as the servant of God and Abraham as a loving father?

6. In the body of the play how does the author use the changes in Abraham's feelings and those in Isaac's feelings to keep the play moving? Discuss the way he counterpoints the feelings of the two characters.

7. Comment on the dramatic irony of Abraham's remark to Isaac in lines 144-46.

8. Describe the climax of the play.

9. What is the purpose of the appearance of the Doctor at the end of the play?

Character

1. What is the effect of Isaac's request that his eyes be covered and that the stroke be delivered quickly?

2. Why does the author show Isaac as afraid of the sword, even after he has been rescued? To what extent is the picture of Isaac as a child convincing?

3. Why does the mother not appear in this play?

The Stage

1. Discuss the effect of Abraham's uncertainty

about the kind of animal to be sacrificed. Here, and in other appropriate places, you might consider the effect of the audience's knowledge of the story on their reactions to the play.

2. Presuming that the play was designed to be performed on a stage somewhat like a flat wagon-bed, determine how many playing areas must be provided and how they might be related to one another vertically and horizontally.

3. The play contains a number of anachronisms, especially the references to the Trinity. What explanation might there be for them?

Symbol and Myth

1. Old Testament stories were selected for use in mystery plays largely because of their foreshadowing of the life of Jesus. Comment on how the father-son relation described here foreshadows the doctrine of Jesus as Son of God offered as a sacrifice in the Crucifixion.

2. What is the relation between the use of the ram and the figure of Jesus as the Lamb of God?

The Author's Works

1. Examine Genesis 22:1-21 to determine what the author found in his source. How did he add to or magnify elements of the story? A reading of the entire story of Abraham in Genesis reveals certain elements of Abraham's life not stressed or included in this play. You might want to consider the effect of a knowledge of the story of Hagar and Ishmael on one's response to the play, for example.

2. We do not know anything about the writer of this play. Can we make any guesses as to whether he was experienced in using owrds either as a writer or a preacher? Do such speculations help us to understand the play better?

William Shakespeare   Hamlet (p. 595)

HAMLET   Do you see yonder cloud that's almost in shape of a camel?
POLONIUS   By the mass, and 'tis like a camel, indeed.
HAMLET   Methinks it is like a weasel.
POLONIUS   It is backed like a weasel.
HAMLET   Or like a whale?
POLONIUS   Very like a whale.

Some of our students, I am afraid, feel as if we are playing Hamlet to their Polonius when we offer a reading or interpretation of a piece of literature, particularly when the work is as complex, awe-inspiring, and, for some, hard to follow and comprehend as Hamlet. It may be useful, then, to put them, individually or jointly, in the position not of Polonius but of Hamlet and ask them, at the beginning of the hour, to write out in twenty-five to a hundred words a summary of the play. In Writing about Literature we have offered three such summaries of Hamlet:

A young man, seeking to avenge the murder of his father by his uncle, kills his uncle, but he himself and others die in the process.

In Denmark, many centuries ago, a young prince avenged the murder of his father, the king, by his uncle, who had usurped the throne, but the prince himself was killed, as were others, and a well-led foreign army had no trouble successfully invading the decayed and troubled state.

From the ghost of his murdered father a young prince learns that his uncle, who had married the prince's mother, much to the young man's shame and disgust, is the father's murderer, and he plots revenge, feigning madness, acting erratically--even to insulting the woman he loves--and, though gaining his revenge, causes the suicide of his beloved and the deaths of others and, finally, of himself.

The first emphasizes the revenge motif, the second adds a political dimension, the third introduces the possible Oedipal overtones. If you are lucky, your twelve, twenty, or thirty-five students will offer camel, weasel, whale, and a whole ark of readings, paired or not. They may cover most of the orthodox and unorthodox ways of looking at the play or at the hero--as an intellectual, a man incapable of decisive action, a man troubled by obesity, a homosexual, or a man too much in love with his mother. There are bound to be a number of different readings, or summaries with differing emphases. It might be profitable to have one read out and ask how many others are similar and group similar ones together, perhaps even asking the students involved to come up with a joint summary. Then you might ask for a summary that seems radically different, have it read and see if that reading has adherents, etc. If there is surprising homogeneity from the beginning there will still be enough to generate useful class discussion in trying to determine the best wording or adding the most essential matters left out, etc.
If you cannot get enough fruitful controversy

going with student summaries, you may want to offer a provocative reading of your own, such as the following, in which Hamlet is seen as a shrewd, ambitious politician whose actions are morally questionable and Claudius not much more than another politician who has eliminated his opponent and is in turn eliminated:

Shakespeare is here concerned with questions of succession to power and the virtues appropriate to private and public persons. Because Hamlet is a prince, he has no real choice about his career, about when he is to become king, about whom he is to marry; Shakespeare and his audience shared these and other notions about the meaning of being a prince. We see Hamlet at a difficult juncture in his life. He has been brought up to rule, and we suspect with Fortinbras that he could be very effective. Yet at the height of his maturity (he is thirty), he has been denied his rightful place. Even before he sees the ghost of his father, Hamlet is behaving in a peculiar manner. He dresses in black and goes about the court with his eyes on the ground, deliberately calling attention to himself and his plight.

In the Shakespearean tragic world, order is the supreme value, and those who sin against it will ultimately be punished. Claudius is the king, Hamlet the subject, and therefore Hamlet's ambition becomes morally ambiguous. He wants to fulfill what he sees as his God-given destiny to become king of Denmark, but to do so he must commit the most disorderly act he can think of, to kill a king. He does not even have the excuse of Bolingbroke in Richard III that the king is doing a bad job. Claudius seems to be an effective ruler, however much Hamlet despises him. Hamlet can justify action against him only if he can prove that the king came to the throne in a criminal way. The appearance of the ghost provides a proof, but it does not answer the crucial question. Does Hamlet have the right to take the law into his own hands and punish the usurper or should he wait for the power that guides the universe to restore order in its own way? Can order be restored by disorderly acts?

Hamlet is a superlative actor, as I believe Shakespeare thinks that every successful public figure must be. The image which the public has of him is as important to him as it is to Claudius, who is afraid to act against him directly because of his popularity. As Hamlet admits to his mother, the ostentatious acts of public mourning are "actions that a man might play." With evidence provided by the ghost as his justification, he then proceeds to act out his perception of the situation for the people. Using the analogy of the king as the head of the body which is the state, he makes his madness into the figure of an illegitimate kingship. The disorder in his head represents the disorder in the kingdom. The plan is so politically skillful that Claudius, the play's other consummate politician-actor, sees through it at once.

The appearance of the actors provides Hamlet with a chance for the even more theatrical coup of the play-within-the-play. He proceeds from metaphor to stage representation, but he chooses to make the murderer the nephew of the king as a warning to Claudius. Again Claudius understands and takes the only action he sees as possible, to arrange the death of Hamlet. The situation reverses itself and Hamlet sees immediately what Claudius has in mind. Throughout the play there is a struggle between two evenly matched politicians which adds to the power of the play.

In addition to the question of succession, the play engages the problem of the relation between private and public virtues. This is done through a series of foils to Hamlet and through the description of his relation to Ophelia. The primary foil is Fortinbras, who like Hamlet is a prince, the son of a dead king. The contrast between him and Hamlet is a problem even to Hamlet himself, and it is Fortinbras who is ultimately able to restore the order and assume the kingship in a proper manner. Fortinbras is more fortunate than Hamlet in two ways: he can curb his ambition, and he is in the right place at the right time. Therefore he succeeds where Hamlet fails. The part of Fortinbras is frequently cut in performances of the play, but that undermines some of what the play says. At the other extreme from Fortinbras are Rosencrantz and Guildenstern, the epitome of the ordinary subjects:

> GUILDENSTERN   On Fortune's cap we are not the very button.
> HAMLET   Nor the soles of her shoes?
> ROSENCRANTZ   Neither, my lord.

They call attention to Hamlet's inability to accept the role of subject. Between these two is Laertes, the person in the play most like Hamlet. They are the same age, both of noble birth. Both have a preference for living away from home, and both are expert fencers. They finally confront each other in Ophelia's grave. Laertes seems very much what Hamlet would have been if he had not been a prince. Finally there is Horatio, the good private man. Hamlet understands his virtue, but knows that it is not for him.

Hamlet's relation to Ophelia also underlines the contrast between private and public virtue. If Hamlet had been a private individual, the play seems to suggest that he and Ophelia would have married. Yet Hamlet chooses to use her for political ends just as if she had meant nothing to him. His public abuse of her in the play-within-a-play scene is shocking, and effective as a sign of madness because it is such an incongruous way for a well-bred prince to treat a virgin of the court, and particularly for this prince to treat this virgin. As in the scene with his mother, Hamlet paints himself as unbelievably callous. Only a man who puts political necessity above everything would do such things.

Questions for Classroom Use

Plot
1. Although the eldest son of the king was customarily chosen to succeed his father, the monarchy of Denmark is depicted in the play as elective. Why was Hamlet passed over in favor of his uncle in the election which preceded the opening of the play?

2. What are the circumstances of Horatio's return to Elsinore from Wittenberg? How does the timing of his arrival contribute to the exposition?

3. Describe Hamlet's behavior, his appearance and actions, before he learns even of the appearance of his father's Ghost. To what action does it prompt Claudius of which we learn in Act 2, Scene 2? Why does the King permit Laertes to return to Paris and at the same time refuse Hamlet's request to return to Wittenberg?

4. Is Hamlet surprised by the revelations of the Ghost?

5. When Rosencrantz and Guildenstern appear, Hamlet correctly interprets the King's strategy in sending for them. Does he see through other moves made by Claudius? What does this suggest about the relation between the two antagonists?

6. Why are the players introduced? Why is the King in the play-within-a-play murdered by his nephew?

7. The climax of the play occurs when the King stops the play-within-a-play. What has Hamlet learned and how does it affect his course of action? How is Claudius affected by events of the scene?

8. What prior actions bring about the death of Polonius? The madness and death of Ophelia? What later actions result from the death of Polonius?

9. What is the purpose in terms of dramatic

structure for the scene between Hamlet and Horatio at the beginning of Act 5, Scene 2?

10. What dramatic functions are served by having both Horatio and Fortinbras alive and on stage at the end of the play?

Character

1. What does Laertes's warning to Ophelia suggest about the character of Hamlet?

2. Hamlet tells his mother in Act 1, Scene 2 that his manner of dress and his deportment are "actions that a man might play." In which scenes does Hamlet seem to be "acting," playing a public role?

3. What issues are presented in Hamlet's soliloquies which can be presented otherwise only with difficulty? Do any of the other characters have soliloquies?

4. Hamlet uses a trick of speech of repeating a word or phrase several times. Do any other characters have individual speech mannerisms? What purpose might such mannerisms serve?

5. From time to time Hamlet makes unfavorable remarks about the King's behavior and appearance. Do the other characters make such remarks? To what extent should Hamlet's remarks influence the choice of an actor to play Claudius?

6. Compare the situation of Hamlet and young Fortinbras at each of the times Fortinbras is mentioned or appears. The character of Fortinbras is frequently omitted in performance. Why is it easy to cut the role? What does such a cut do to the play?

7. As his death approaches, Hamlet asks Horatio, first, to see that his actions and death are properly reported and, second, to use Hamlet's name and posthumous influence to bring about the election of Fortinbras as king. How is the order of the two requests significant?

The Stage

1. The Shakespearean stage featured a large central acting area around which members of the audience sat or stood, on three sides. In addition there were, very probably, an elevated area above the main stage, a recessed area upstage, and one or more trap doors. If you were staging Hamlet on such a stage, how would you treat the various scenes? What use would you make of the subsidiary acting areas?

2. As a member of the company which performed his plays, Shakespeare seems to have written a part for a particular actor on occasion. What part in Hamlet might have been written for a specialist in sententious old men? for a specialist in effeminate young men? for another kind of specialist? Are there

scenes in which the actor's part seems to have been lengthened or emphasized in order to take advantage of his specialty?

3. In several speeches Hamlet talks about the theatrical practices of the period and the purposes of the drama. To what extent, if any, can we assume that Hamlet's comments represent Shakespeare's own ideas? What are some of the particular abuses which Hamlet cites? Have they disappeared from theatrical practice?

4. One common theatrical practice was the use of boys who had not reached puberty to play women's parts. Does Hamlet refer to this? How would such a practice affect the writing of a play? of this particular play?

5. When the play ends, what should be the position of Hamlet's body relative to the other actors? How does it compare with his relative position at his first appearance?

Symbol and Myth

1. A central image in the play is the comparison between the body and the state, the "body politic." Such an image pattern assumes an analogy between two levels of reality, the body and the state. One occurrence of the image is in the Ghost's account to Hamlet of his death by having poison poured in his ear and of the report of his death as an abuse of the ear of Denmark. Can you find others? In terms of the image of the body politic, why does Hamlet choose to feign madness?

2. There are a number of references in the play to warfare and weapons and to hunting, fishing, and trapping. Do these constitute meaningful image patterns which contribute to the internal complexity of the work? Are there other such groups of references?

The Author's Works

1. In a number of his plays Shakespeare seems to be commenting on the relation between virtues appropriate to public life and those appropriate to private life. In some cases--for example, Brutus in Julius Caesar--they seem so distinct as to be irreconcilable. Laertes seems to touch on this issue in his advice to Ophelia. Are there other places where it is treated? What does the play say about the distinction?

Genre

1. Some writing about tragedy talks about the concept of hamartia, the notion that the central character's fate is brought about by a tragic flaw or failing of character. Hamlet's speech beginning "So

oft it chanceth in particular men" suggests something similar. Does Hamlet have such a tragic flaw? If so, name it and write a paper supporting your contention.

2. Another idea common in writing about tragedy is that the hero is guilty of <u>hubris</u>, an overstepping of the bounds of his destiny and the destiny of man. This suggests some universal moral principles beyond the control of men. Are such principles assumed in the play? If so, what are they and how does Hamlet overstep them?

Historical Setting
1. In 1600 (the approximate date of <u>Hamlet</u>) Queen Elizabeth I was 67 and had no direct heirs. England had been subjected to wars and rebellions over the succession to the throne for the preceding two centuries. How are these historical circumstances reflected in <u>Hamlet</u>?

3 CHARACTER AND ACTOR

Henrik Ibsen   <u>Hedda</u> <u>Gabler</u> (p. 695)

Questions for Classroom Use

Plot
1. The scenes between Hedda and Loevborg then Hedda, Mrs. Elvsted, and Loevborg in Act II are central to the themes of cowardice and courage. Define the quality of Hedda's cowardice and Mrs. Elvsted's courage and how they find expression in Loevborg.

2. Why is Loevborg upset when Hedda reveals Mrs. Elvsted's concerns for him in the city?

3. What does Hedda mean when she says that Loevborg will return with a "crown of vine-leaves in his hair. Burning and unshamed"?

4. Act III concludes with the burning of Loevborg's manuscript, and with that action earlier references to "burning" resonate with new meaning. Examine these references and images, especially when later George is shocked by Hedda's apparent ardor, surprised that "you're burning with love for me, Hedda."

5. Compare and contrast Hedda's envy of Mrs. Elvsted and George's envy of Loevborg. How do they conflate in the identification of the manuscript as Loevborg's and Thea's "child"?

6. Why does Hedda insist that Loevborg end his life "beautifully"?

7. Act IV opens on a note of formal mourning. In the course of the act which characters die and what responses do their deaths elicit from the others?

8. Hedda protests Brack's hold over her because she is "not free." What freedom does Hedda require and how does she employ it?

9. Brack's last line is an echo of Hedda's when she tells Mrs. Elvsted that "People don't do such things" regarding Loevborg's mystery woman who shot at him. How is the echo meaningful?

10. Is Hedda's suicide an act of cowardice or courage? What is your reaction to it?

Character

1. Characterize George Tesman. How can he be distinguished from the caricatured absent-minded professor of a comic farce? What is revealed by his constant punctuation of sentences with "What?"

2. Hedda later admits to Judge Brack the she purposefully mistook Miss Tesman's hat for Bertha's. What in Hedda's character accounts for this cruelty? Why does Hedda behave in such an aloof manner to her new relative?

3. In her refusal to call Miss Tesman "Auntie Juju," Hedda is maintaining strict formality much as one would in addressing a friend or relation by "vous" instead of "tu" in French. Examine other occasions when the use of informal names is important, as when Hedda mistakenly remembers Thea's name as Tora, becomes upset when Loevborg calls her Hedda, and finally addresses George by his Christian name.

4. Hedda is amazed by Mrs. Elvsted's open break with social conformity in deserting her husband. What are Hedda's attitudes toward society and the appearance that she makes in that society?

5. The first act ends with the apparent revelation that Hedda is the woman from Loevborg's past. What does this tell us about Hedda that we did not already know? What new expectation does it arouse?

6. Why is Hedda so intrigued by the "competition" between George and Loevborg? Why does Judge Brack find the competition suited to his purposes?

7. What purpose does the opening scene of Act II serve besides making Judge Brack's intentions perfectly obvious? What new information do we learn? What does it tell us about Hedda's character? Why does the scene open with a pistol shot?

8. Hedda complains to Judge Brack of her honeymoon that she went six months "without even meeting a single person who was one of us, and to

whom I could talk about the kind of things we talk about." What kind of things do they talk about? Distinguish the layers of Hedda's boredom with the world.

9. Characterize Loevborg. What are his strengths? his weaknesses? How are they related?

10. Why is George so shocked at the subject of Loevborg's new book? How are their approaches to their professions and to life different? How is it that Hedda is involved with two such different men?

11. Why did Hedda draw out Loevborg and act as his "confessor" when they were young? Why does Loevborg mistake it for love?

12. When Hedda suggests to George that Loevborg is "less afraid of life than most men," George responds, "Good heavens, no. He just doesn't know the meaning of the word moderation." Whose assessment is more accurate? Is this moment of insight consistent with George's character?

13. Discuss Judge Brack's character and his role in the action of the play. What segment of society does he represent? What segments do Hedda, George, and Loevborg represent? What qualities or abilities does the judge possess that allow him to create the "triangle"?

14. Does Mrs. Elvsted's inspiration of George and her plans to move in with Miss Tesman complete a new triangle excluding Hedda? What does Hedda's imitation of George in the last scene ("Fancy that, by Jove!") indicate regarding this turn of events?

The Stage

1. The portrait of Hedda's father, General Gabler, often dominates the set in productions of Hedda Gabler. Why is the portrait given such a central position in the set, and how is the general's "presence" important to the play's action?

2. Miss Tesman drops some broad hints about Hedda's pregnancy early in the play. How obvious are they in the text and how obvious should they be in production?

Arthur Miller   <u>Death</u> <u>of</u> a <u>Salesman</u> (p. 765)

If you have been discussing this play in class in terms of language, there are a few aspects not covered in the chapter that you may want to pursue, such as the function of repetition (even of seemingly insignificant phrases), the allegorical potential of names in this seemingly realistic play, the implications and appropriateness of the title, the efficacy or reliability of language within the play. Perhaps such concerns may be put in the form of questions or suggestions:

1. The play is filled with oft-repeated phrases such as "well liked," "the woods are burning," "I'm going to lose weight"; what others can you find? What general purpose do these repetitions serve? Does each have a specific purpose?

2. To what extent are the names "Loman" ("low man"?) and "Singleman" allegorical? There is another "man," the one in the title--"Salesman"; to which death of which salesman does the title refer? Could you make a case for its referring to both? (Note: Singleman dies at the midpoint of the play; he has been held up as an ideal by Loman.) One of Miller's working titles for this play was <u>In His Head</u>. In what ways would this be an appropriate title? Is this or <u>Death</u> <u>of</u> a <u>Salesman</u> the better title?

3. In Act I Willy describes himself as "fat," "foolish to look at," and a man who "talks too much," which does not fit his own philosophy of success. How does he reconcile the two? What, if anything, does he do to make aims and reality coincide? How does the contradiciton reflect on his words? his beliefs?

4. Why are Willy's interview suggestions to Biff so contradictory? Does Willy follow his own advice in his interview with Howard Wagner?

You may also want to ask about the difference between language and performance by focusing on the stage directions. When we read the play, for example, we learn of Happy that "Sexuality is like a visible color on him, or a scent that many women have discovered." How do you get that across in performance? (Spray the theatre with musk?) Is there a universal color-scent, acting style, or even appearance that would do? Sexuality or "sex appeal" may not mean the same thing to everyone. Most of us, no doubt, can understand why Arthur Miller was attracted sexually to Marilyn Monroe, whom he married, but can we all understand what Monroe saw in Miller?

If your classes are anything like mine they will not wait until Chapter 6 to use the word "tragedy," and, without stepping all over the grass, you might be able to introduce the term "pathos" and allow the discussion to pursue the question as to whether Salesman is pathetic or tragic. Linda's evaluation of Willy and his situation is quoted in the chapter: "He's not the finest character that even lived. But he's a human being, and a terrible thing is happening to him. So attention must be paid . . ."; this is perhaps the basis on which one might want to argue about the possibility of a "tragedy of the common man," and of course the discussion would double back to the use of common rather than elevated language. Most definitions of tragedy also involve the "hero's" recognition of himself and his situation, so that Biff's claim in the Requiem that Willy "never knew who he was" would have to be evaluated in terms of the text. Finally, the Greek gods may be here replaced by "society." To what extent is Willy the victim of his society, that is, more specifically, of capitalism?

Whether you come to it through discussion of tragedy or not, you surely will want to have your students take a look at what seems to be suggested about modern American society, its nature, values, state of health, effect on human beings and their values, relationship to reality or nature. You might want to get things started by asking such questions as these:

1. The play is set in post-World War II New York City, while the flashbacks take place in 1928. Why should Willy choose precisely the year 1928 to recall?
2. Biff seems driven to steal. Why? What personal or family reasons are there? What, if any, societal reasons?
3. Willy seems constantly badgered by machines (his cars, the washer, the refrigerator, the wire recorder, etc.), yet Charley remarks that Willy was "a happy man with a batch of cement," and Willy himself desperately wants to grow things and laments that "I don't have a thing in the ground." What positive and negative values are suggested by these details? How do they relate to the vocation of "selling"?

It is hard to imagine two works more different from each other than <u>Death of a Salesman</u> and <u>A Rose for Emily</u> but a comparison of the two either as "elegies" or as stories suggesting the clash of cultures or generations might make a good paper topic. You may have noticed that the Requiem makes no mention of the twenty thousand dollars in insurance money. What do your students think would have happened to it? Perhaps a comparison of this play and <u>The Rocking Horse Winner</u>, centering on money, would make a good paper topic.

Like much drama, from <u>Oedipus</u> to <u>Hamlet</u> to <u>Hedda Gabler</u> and on and on and on, <u>Salesman</u> significantly, though not necessarily centrally, concerns parent(s) and child(ren). It should not take much to get your students to talk about parents, their weaknesses, imperfections, responsibilities, but you may want to hang out some bait, like the question about why Biff steals, or why Happy just can't help seducing executives' girl friends. Willy claims Biff ruined his own life to spite his father; Biff claims Willy filled him with hot air. Who is right? How much responsibility lies where? You may, indeed, want to begin with the family character and conflict (even bringing in Uncle Ben, perhaps), and only later, when righteousness and deflected guilt are exhausted, or lying like a patient etherized upon a table, descend to the more particular, pedantic, and poetic element of language.

The set design, lighting, and music are all key elements in the production of <u>Salesman</u>, and you may want to lead your students through a discussion of how these can contribute to the movement, effect, and even meaning of the play. Jo Mielziner, who designed the scenes, writes informatively of the problems, intent, and solutions in <u>Designing for the Theatre</u> (New York: Atheneum, 1965), and you may want to tell your students about the initial production or you may ask that one or more students read and report on the issues discussed in that book.

More readily available for full class discussion is the device of the flashback, not only the meaning but the structure. All stories have a past, but in most plays the "necessary" past is supplied by exposition. You may want to ask you students how Miller may have used exposition to tell his story, perhaps asking them to reduce one or another of the flashback scenes to exposition of various kinds (not just the narration of a past scene such as Willy's description of Biff on the football field). Perhaps more interesting would be to ask that one or more <u>Salesman</u>-like flashbacks be written for <u>Hedda Gabler</u> (Hedda and her father the General, for instance) or

<u>Oedipus</u> or <u>Streetcar</u>.

   <u>A Soldier's Play</u>, like <u>Salesman</u>, uses the
flashback rather extensively. You may want to ask
your students to compare how and why the device is
used in the two plays.

Sophocles   Oedipus Tyrannus (p. 840)

Our students are faced with an uncertain world,
and we see them groping toward contemporary oracles.
Time and again they are forced to choose between
equally unpalatable alternatives, without being able
to find comfort in the knowledge that everything is
foreordained, whether by the stars, or by a Calvinist
God, or by the moira (fate) which rules the life of
Oedipus.

In a different way, Oedipus was faced with such
a situation when he visited the oracle at Delphi
before the play begins. Informed that his fate was to
kill his father and marry his mother, he saw two
alternatives--to return home and realize his moira or
to refuse to accept his destiny. When he decided on
the latter, he refused to accept the limitations of
his mortality, a refusal called hubris by Aristotle
in the first definition of tragedy. What happens to
Oedipus as a result of his choice is an education in
human limitation.

Nothing in the play is more theatrical and more
significant than the contrast between Oedipus as he
first appears and Oedipus as he appears at the end of
the play. The first scene has a ceremonial or
heiratic quality. The Chorus of Theban Elders is
lamenting the plague when Oedipus appears and asks
what is going on. He knows the answer because he has
already sent Creon to Delphi for help. The question
is part of a ceremony in which the King (or Tyrant,
as the Greeks called him, using the word differently)
allows his subjects to make requests of him and
promises to help them. He sees himself as a king, a
god on earth. He has conquered the Sphinx; surely he
can conquer the plague.

What Oedipus does not realize is that beneath
his royal robes there is only "a poor, bare, forked
animal," as Lear discovered. The Greek audience was
constantly reminded of this because Oedipus' name,
which means "swollen-footed," reminds us that when he
was a baby, "Laius [his father] drove pins into his
ankles before sending him to die of exposure." We do
not know how the Greeks represented his wound on
stage, but there must have been some reminder of his
physical infirmity.

Forgetful of his infirmity, the reminder of his
mortality, Oedipus must learn again that he is human.
Coming to Thebes as a young man, he had saved the
city by killing the Sphinx. He had been acclaimed as
king and married Jocasta, an older woman, but a queen

and still presumably beautiful and sexually responsive. Over the years his reign has been happy and his marriage fruitful. He is the man who has everything, but he has come to believe that his success and happiness are the result of his own choices. The fact that the Elders want him to save the city from the plague suggests that they believe he can do so, and Oedipus also believes that he can.

The body of the play recounts the steps by which Oedipus comes to realize, as the Chorus points out at the end, that "none of us mortals can truly be thought of as happy . . . until he is dead and must suffer no more." At first, proud and forgetful of his humanity, Oedipus intitiates his own downfall with his promise to the people, "I shall not cease until I bring the truth to light. . . . I shall not rest till I dispel this defilement." At this point Creon has returned with the message of the oracle that the murderer of Laius must be punished. If Oedipus had asked the right questions, he might have discovered the truth at this point, but the dramatic movement depends on the tension between discovery and the failure to react properly to that discovery. The dramatic effect is further intensified by the use of dramatic irony, as in Oedipus' speech in which he swears, essentially, to drive himself out of Thebes without understanding the true meaning of what he is saying. The dramatic irony is intensified when Oedipus says that he must punish the murderer of Laius lest the murderer of one king should move against a second. He does not understand that his oath insures that Oedipus, the murderer of Laius, must punish himself for that act.

The second discovery is made by Teiresias, and it is not ambiguous. Teiresias tells Oedipus that he (Oedipus) is the murderer, but again Oedipus refuses to understand. He sees Teiresias' statement as part of a conspiracy led by Creon. We see in this attack something of the insecurity which Oedipus feels in relation to his wife and her brother, who are, after all, older, more experienced, and natives of Thebes. The resulting quarrel between Oedipus and Creon brings Jocasta to the stage. Jocasta is an interesting character: she does not believe in oracles because, as she tells us, an oracle had said that Laius would be murdered by his own son. Oedipus does not make the connection with what the oracle had told him. He resists discovery again, instead focusing on the question of whether Laius had been murdered by a "robber" or "robbers" at the place where three roads met.

The next discovery is that of the First Messenger, who comes to tell Oedipus that his father is dead, but instead tells him that his parentage is unknown. Jocasta understands and leaves the stage to kill herself, but Oedipus yet again resists discovery. He fears that his unknown birth means that Jocasta "feels shame for my humble birth." Jocasta has tried to prevent Oedipus from his search for the truth, but he moves forward to the inevitable revelation. In the moment before the final discovery Oedipus finally understands.

> SHEPHERD   Ah, master, do I <u>have</u> to speak?
> OEDIPUS   You have to. And I <u>have</u> to hear.

After the ultimate revelation the play moves rapidly to its conclusion. Jocasta has killed herself, Oedipus has put out his own eyes, and Creon is left to rule, however unwillingly.

At the end of the play Oedipus appears again, deposed, self-blinded, self-exiled from the native city in which he had felt himself a stranger. At the beginning of the play Oedipus was different from other people because he was happy, successful, and powerful. Now he is different because of his overweening pride and the crimes which he has committed because of it. Yet Oedipus is a tragic figure because he has learned to hate his crimes but not to hate himself. He might have chosen to kill himself, following Jocasta's example, but the fact that he does not expresses his basic dignity, his acceptance of himself and his humanity.

Questions for Classroom Use

Plot

1. Does Oedipus already know what the Priest "tells" him in the opening exchange with the Priest? If he does, why is the scene included? How might it be staged to make it more plausible?

2. How does Oedipus react to the message which Creon brings from the oracle at Delphi? Does he have any other motive for his decision to seek Laius' murderers than his desire to rid the city of plague? Why had there been no earlier search for the murderer of Laius?

3. Why do the members of the Chorus, in their first ode, say, "I quake and I dread and I tremble at these words," when, in fact, the response of the oracle implies a solution to their problems?

4. What dramatic device is used in Oedipus' oath to avenge the murderer of Laius? How does the choice of the words used reinforce the dramatic effect? The story of Oedipus would have been familiar to the Athenian audience. How might this knowledge have

affected their reaction to Oedipus' oath?

5. What is Teiresias' initial response to the summons and questions of response? What does he finally tell Oedipus? Why does Oedipus not believe him?

6. Why does Oedipus suspect Creon of plotting to gain the throne of Thebes? How is this related to Oedipus' later assumption that Jocasta is upset about the possibility that Oedipus may be of low birth?

7. Why does Jocasta tell Oedipus what she knows about the death of Laius? How does Oedipus react to the various details of her account? Does he ignore any important ones?

8. Why does Oedipus begin his account of his adventure at the place where three roads meet with an account of what happened to him in Corinth and at the oracle in Delphi? How does Jocasta react? Does she suspect anything out of the ordinary?

9. What is the reaction of the Chorus to this scene between Oedipus and Jocasta? Why does the ode end with the chorus figuratively turning its back on oracles?

10. What news does Messenger 1 bring? What revelation is brought about by it? How do Oedipus, Jocasta, and the Chorus react?

11. Why is one shepherd both the man who escaped from the murder of Laius and the one who was to have exposed the infant Oedipus to death? Does Oedipus ever clear up the question of the number of "robbers" involved in Laius' death?

12. Comment on the dramatic impact of this exchange:

SHEPHERD   Ah, master, do I have to speak?
OEDIPUS   You have to. And I have to hear.

13. Referring to his self-blinding, Oedipus says that Apollo "brought this pain, this suffering to me. But it was my own hand that struck the blow." How does this statement also refer to the entire tragedy of Oedipus?

Character
1. What elements of Oedipus' character caused him to go to Delphi after Polybus and Merope had denied the story that he was not their son? Do the same elements work in his actions in the play?

2. What parts of Oedipus' downfall come from his own character? Which ones come from the circumstances of his life? Is there evidence in what we know of Laius and Jocasta that Oedipus' guilt might be in part inherited?

The Stage
1. Since the opening scene is a public ceremony

of sorts, how should Oedipus be dressed? Would his appearance in full royal regalia be appropriate? How would such an appearance add to the impact of the final scene?

2. This play was written to be performed by only three actors. Which roles would have been performed by each of the three, assuming that no two actors played the same role?

3. Why does the chorus consist of the elders of Thebes? What part do they play in the action? How is the content of their choral odes related to the action around each ode?

4. How does the actual time of performance relate to the amount of time required by the events of the play? How is the passage of time indicated?

Symbol and Myth

1. There are a number of references in the play to blindness and sight and to light and darkness. Find some of them and examine the use of the group of images.

2. What is the significance of the fact that Apollo, the sun god, is also a god of prophecy? Why is Teiresias, as a prophet inspired by Apollo, presented as blind?

The Author's Work

1. In comparison with his younger contemporary Euripides, Sophocles in his best-known plays seems generally to favor the status quo and the powers-that-be. Can you see evidence of this in Oedipus Tyrannus?

Genre

1. The terms hubris and hamartia are frequently used in discussions of tragedy. How are they relevant to the story of Oedipus?

2. How does the account of Oedipus' search for the murderer of Laius resemble a detective story? What makes it different?

Historical Setting

1. What view of the gods and their decrees is presented in the play? Does the fact that the oracle has said that Oedipus will kill his father and marry his mother absolve him of guilt in doing so? If not, why not?

Oscar Wilde   The Importance of Being Earnest (p. 869)

At the heart of the play is the basic comedic

plot: a young man and a young woman wish to marry. Some difficulty is interposed which renders the union seemingly impossible, but then the difficulty is removed and all live happily ever after. The plot here is double, for there are two young men and two young women: the romance of the second pair is triggered by the complications of the romance of the first pair and resolved by the resolution of those complications. This is the heart of comedy, for the typical comedic plot is concerned with someone who is denied his or her rightful place in society, but who ultimately overcomes the denial. In comedy—as opposed to such forms as farce—marriage is viewed in its social aspect rather than its sexual one. The concern is with the wedding rather than the wedding night, and therefore the surface unconcern with sexuality works. Many other comedies overlap into the area of sexuality but not _Earnest_; it stays strictly within the proper domain of comedy. Jack and Algernon are eminently suitable to be husbands except that Jack has no parents and Algernon no money, and those two characteristics are important in marriage in its social aspect. As healthy young women, Gwendolen and Cecily are admirably suited for marriage and motherhood, and we feel that it is well that difficulties are so expeditiously resolved.

While it is a perfect comedy, _Earnest_ also exemplifies the narrower genre called the comedy of manners. The comedy of manners differs from other comedies in its emphasis on life among the wealthy, with people who "toil not, neither do they spin." Their concerns are those of high society rather than of society in the general sense. Algernon, for example, is deeply concerned with such burning issues as who his dinner partner will be or what music is to be performed at a party. The values of such people may seem superficial to many people, including today's students, but if nothing else, these serve to make the play even more amusing. That Wilde himself understood this is clear in the brilliantly funny interrogation of Jack by Lady Bracknell. Throughout we are confronted with a comic inversion of values. When Lady Bracknell inquires whether he smokes, he hesitantly replies that he does, delighted because she thinks a man should have some occupation. Lady Bracknell, as a senior matron, is one of the controlling forces of society, who can change either the fashion or the side, or both, if necessary. Her values are totally consistent and totally inverted from our perspective, and their inversion gives them much of their humor.

The play is also a brilliant example of the artful use of comic stereotypes. Jack and Gwendolen are representative of such "witty lovers" as Beatrice and Benedick in <u>Much Ado about Nothing</u> and Mirabell and Millamant in <u>The Way of the World</u>. Algernon and Cecily are "sentimental lovers." Miss Prism is an old maid, anxious to marry Canon Chasuble, a slightly dim clergyman, and Lady Bracknell the managing matron. Yet though all are "stereotypes," Wilde succeeds in giving each of them more than enough individuality to maintain our interest in them. For example, Algernon is portrayed throughout the play as being excessively interested in food, not a usual trait in a sentimental lover.

The glory of the play is as much in its language as in its structure and characterization, for Wilde was a master wit. Some of the devices which he uses are worth examination. One is the non sequitur, as in Algernon's remark to Lane: "Speaking of the science of Life, have you got the cucumber sandwiches cut for Aunt Augusta?" That the connection between the science of Life (whatever that is) and cucumber sandwiches is at best tenuous is the source of the humor here as in other places. A second technique is the use of the unexpected word. When Lane mentions his marriage, Algernon is shocked because "Really, if the lower orders don't set us a good example, what on earth is the use of them?" The question would not be funny if he had said "upper" instead of "lower," but the unexpected word provides the humor. Another form of humor is the use of rhetorical balance and parallelism, as in Jack's remark that "When one is in town one amuses oneself. When one is in the country one amuses other people." Puns may be the lowest form of humor (and then again they may not), but Wilde uses them brilliantly, as in the title of the play, which leads to the final line. Another form of humor is the establishment of apparently logical categories which have no real meaning, as when Algernon explains why he does not intend to have dinner with his aunt. "To begin with, I dined there on Monday. . . . In the second place, whenever I do dine there I am always treated as a member of the family. . . . In the third place, I know perfectly well whom she will place me next to." A final form of humor is the use of speeches which clearly contradict facts, as when Gwendolen, replying to her mother's command to go into the next room with her, answers, "Certainly mamma," and remains behind. These examples could be multiplied many times from other sections of the play.

Questions for Classroom Use

Plot

1. What is the purpose of the opening exchange between Algernon and Lane?

2. What do we learn about the opening situation of the play from the conversation between Algernon and Jack? How does Wilde use the cigarette case for expository and comic purposes?

3. What does Algernon offer Jack in exchange for a free dinner? How does he fulfill his share of the agreement? What plot complication results from it?

4. How does Lady Bracknell react to the news of Gwendolen's engagement to Jack? What does her maternal interrogation of Jack tell us about her values and those of her society?

5. How does Wilde make use of the fact that Jack was found in a handbag? What further information do we get from Miss Prism early in Act 2 which contributes to the solution of the play's problems?

6. Why does Algernon suggest that Jack's brother died of chill rather than of apoplexy? What use is made of this later in the play?

7. How does Algernon discover the address of Jack's country place? How has Jack attempted earlier to keep it secret?

8. What bargain does Jack offer to Lady Bracknell? How does she react? What might have happened if the problem had not been resolved?

9. Describe the steps by which the problems are resolved by the appearance of Miss Prism, including any new misunderstanding which may have arisen.

10. Are we prepared for the embrace of Miss Prism and canon Chasuble? If not, why do we accept it?

11. What is the meaning of the final line of the play?

Character

1. Certain of the characters in this play have names which suggest something about their characters. Of which ones is this true, and what do we learn about each from the name?

2. Why does Gwendolen insist that Jack make a formal proposal of marriage?

3. In the opening scene of Act 2 what conclusions does the audience reach about the attitudes and relative intelligence of Miss Prism and Cecily?

4. Why is Miss Prism shown misunderstanding the meaning of the allusion to Egeria?

5. Describe the relation between the attitudes of Gwendolen and Cecily and what they actually say in the opening scene of Act 3.

Patterned Language

1. The last part of Act 2, the scenes between Gwendolen and Cecily, then between them and the two young men, and finally between the two young men, are full of examples of syntactic and rhetorical balance and parallelism. Describe the effect of this device.

2. Compare Lady Bracknell's examination of Cecily in Act 3 with her interrogation of Jack in Act 1. What accounts for the similarities and differences?

3. A good bit of the humor in this play, and a good bit of the meaning, depends on the contrast between appearance and reality. For example, in the first exchange of the play Algernon asks Lane if he has heard what Algernon was playing on the piano. What are we to make of Lane's reply that "I didn't think it polite to listen, sir"? Can you find other examples of this phenomenon? What do they tell us about the meaning of the play?

4. The play uses a number of devices of language and logic for comic purposes. Several are listed below with an example of each. Can you find other examples of each and describe why they are funny and why they add to the meaning of the play?

a. Non sequitur
ALGERNON   Please don't touch the cucumber sandwiches. They are ordered especially for Aunt Augusta. [Takes one and eats it.]
JACK   Well, you have been eating them all the time.
ALGERNON   That is quite a different matter. She is my aunt.

b. Unexpected word
ALGERNON   I hear her hair has turned quite gold from grief.

c. Parallelism
LADY BRACKNELL   To lose one parent, Mr. Worthing, may be regarded as a misfortune; to lose both looks like carelessness.

d. Pun
JACK   It is very vulgar to talk like a dentist when one isn't a dentist. It makes a false impression.
ALGERNON   Well, that is exactly what dentists always do.

Symbol and Myth
1. There are numerous references to food and drink; find examples of them and comment on their meaning in the play.

2. How does Wilde make use of diaries as a structural and comic device in the play?

Genre
1. The typical plot of comedy involves a person blocked from fulfilling the appropriate social role and the removal of the block leading to reconciliation to that role. How does this plot work in The Importance of Being Earnest?
2. Many comic characters are based on stereotyped patterns of character development, such as witty lovers, sentimental lovers, old maids, and managing matrons. Describe their use in this play.
3. The Importance of Being Earnest is an example of the comedy of manners, which portrays people who live on unearned income, which describes the values of such people rather than those of society in general, and which depends heavily on verbal wit. How does this play show those characteristics?

Historical Setting
1. What do the reactions of Miss Prism and Canon Chasuble suggest about the values of conventional moralists? What do the Canon's remarks about his sermon on "the meaning of the manna in the wilderness" suggest about institutional religion?

Samuel Beckett   Krapp's Last Tape (p. 918)

Krapp's Last Tape is obviously a very demanding play for the one actor in it; everything in the play really depends upon the ability of the actor to convey, through quite limited dialogue and quite carefully described gestures and stage business, a complicated and rich sense of character. It is a hard play to act out in class; besides the requirement of highly developed acting skills, it depends very heavily on timing, gestures, and other features that go beyond simply speaking the dialogue, so that even skilled actors need a lot of practice to get matters right. Besides, the age of the character makes him difficult to impersonate for typical college-age students. You may be able to work on a small discrete problem--how, for example, does the character sing out "spool" over and over?--but for the most part you will probably need to discuss this play without being able to rely on extensive class readings of dialogue.
Instead, try to work out of the extensive stage directions. Have your students go into detail about what every single detail is meant to convey--the clothes, item by item; the pockets, the watch; the facial features; the unshaven face; the failed

eyesight, hearing, and voice; the walk; the bananas;
the whole mechanism of tapes; the lighter, the cork,
the ledger, etc. Beckett's stage directions are as
detailed as Williams's, but they explain less fully
what each signifies, and they seldom have symbolic
overtones. Beckett seems to go out of his way to make
every detail individualistic and untypical,
dissociating his character from expectable human
patterns. What does this suggest about the different
aims of Beckett and Tennessee Williams?

Beckett is also anxious to establish the
"artifice" of the play, that is, to keep the audience
aware that they are seeing a play on a stage, not a
slice of natural life. Note, for example, how he has
Krapp self-consciously kick the banana peel into the
orchestra pit at the beginning. What other self-
conscious devices emphasize this fictitiousness?

A good class discussion--or a good paper--can be
developed on the play's preoccupation with time. Ask
your students to sort out, in a particular section of
the play, as precisely as they can how much time is
bridged in the tapes. Insist that they provide
textual evidence. Other topics for discussion that
will enhance an understanding of the play's themes
and effects: how the stage is to be lighted, the
importance of the time of day (in relation to the
issue of Krapp's age), the effects of silence in the
various places, but especially at the end.

Marsha Norman   Third and Oak: The Laundromat (p.
    926)

The drama section begins with Harold in the
milkbar and ends with Marsha in the laundromat--two
short pieces about rather ordinary, not to say common
people in extraordinarily ordinary, most unglamorous
and untheatrical public places, speaking in
ostensibly undistinguished language. The two serve as
bookends, as it were, and can clearly bear
comparison, and the Laundromat is perfect for a final
exam question. Or it can be used to supplement the
first chapter, or to form a unit of short plays with
the Pinter, Chekhov, The Sacrifice of Isaac, and the
Beckett.

Nothing happens on the stage in Third and Oak
and in that it bears comparison with The Black and
White, but whereas the Pinter implies little besides
the mundane emptiness of the two characters' lives,
the Norman play not only defines the emptiness or
loneliness but implies two stories of crises in two
lives. Pinter's characters seem to me almost
indistinguishable--and, indeed, one point he may be

making is that at the fringes of subsistence and margins of city life, people are virtually indistinguishable--but Alberta and Deedee are quite distinct. Even Joe and Harold, who never appear, have enough distinctiveness to talk about or even to write about. Marsha Norman is particularly good at using a fixed scene, very few characters, and virtually no action on stage while, through what in another playwright we might call exposition, creating whole life-stories or life-situations that in other plays would be the staged drama itself. (See how she does it at greater length in 'night, Mother. We chose not to include that longer play, by the way, on the grounds that it might not be too good an idea nowadays to face groups of eighteen- or nineteen-year-olds with stories about suicide.)

If you want to talk about these two plays (or this sketch and play) in class, however, I would suggest grabbing another handle--tone. Do your students find anything funny in The Black and the White? Do we laugh with or at the characters? How about the humor in Third and Oak? Do your students find Pinter's old dears pathetic? Could they describe their daily lives? invent their histories? Is the Pinter more funny or sad? How about the Norman play? It begins with a pratfall and ends with talk of death, loneliness, loss, and all in a few pages. Do students find that disturbing?

Biographical Sketches

SAMUEL BECKETT (1906-   )

Irish by birth, French by adoption and adaptation, Beckett is one of the leading influences in the theatre of the absurd. Although also a novelist and poet of note, he is best known for his highly innovative and often puzzling and controversial plays, which, though often comic confront metaphysical and existential problems and probe the relationship between language and meaning. His most productive years were in the 1950s when he not only wrote three of his best-known novels-- Molloy, Malone Dies, and The Unnamable, but three of his best-known plays as well--the renowned/notorious Waiting for Godot in 1953 and, later in the decade, Endgame and Krapp's Last Tape. More recently Beckett has written shorter, stranger, and less well-received plays, including "Breath" in 1970, which was thirty seconds long and contained no words and no actors. His most recent Broadway play, Rockaby (1981), is a fifteen-minute piece about a woman in a rocking chair reliving her life.

ANTON CHEKHOV (1860-1904)

Chekhov was born at Taganrog where his father, a former serf, owned a grocery store. Later his father went bankrupt and the family moved to Moscow. As early as 1880 Chekhov began writing to earn extra money to help support the family. He gained his early fame as a writer of short fiction, and his work has influenced many later writers of short stories and novellas. In 1884 he graduated in medicine from the University of Moscow and began to practice medicine. Although he had written plays earlier, it was not until 1896 that Chekhov wrote The Seagull, the first of the great plays associated with his name. In 1897 he became seriously ill with tuberculosis, and during the last years of his life he lived at Yalta in the Crimea because of its more healthful climate. In 1901 he married Olga Knipper, an actress of the Moscow Art Theatre who had created several roles in his plays.

HENRIK IBSEN (1828-1906)

Ibsen's theatrical career began in association with the theatres of Bergen and Christiania in his native Norway. In addition to presenting plays of other writers, he produced a number of his own early plays, mostly poetic, historical, and romantic. The most important of these plays were <u>Peer Gynt</u> and <u>Brand</u>. With <u>The Pillar of Society</u> in 1877 he began to write, in prose, a series of realistic problem plays on contemporary subjects, which was to include <u>Ghosts</u> and <u>A Doll's House</u> and which won him international fame. During the last part of his life he lived mainly in Germany and Italy. With <u>The Wild Duck</u> in 1884 he turned to penetrating psychological studies and to increasing use of symbolism. These plays, including <u>Hedda Gabler</u> and <u>The Master Builder</u>, contributed strongly to his enduring reputation.

ARTHUR MILLER   (1915-   )

With the successes of <u>All My Sons</u> (1947) and <u>Death of a Salesman</u> (1949), his second and third professionally produced plays, Arthur Miller established himself as one of the outstanding American playwrights of recent years. Although he has never been prolific, Miller has continued to write steadily for the theatre. His later plays, with the exception of <u>The Price</u> (1968), have not repeated the popular successes of the earlier works, but several of them, including <u>The Crucible</u> (1953) and <u>A View from the Bridge</u> (1955) have been frequently revived with success. His latest play, <u>The American Clock</u>, was produced in 1980. In the same year he wrote the moving and controversial television film <u>Playing for Time</u>, about an actress/musician in a German concentration camp who survives her ordeal by entertaining German officers. <u>Death of a Salesman</u> was awarded the Pulitzer Prize, the Critics Circle Award, and the Antoinette Perry Award, and in 1984 Miller wrote <u>Salesman in Beijing</u> about his own experience in directing a Chinese production of his most famous play.

MARSHA NORMAN (1947-   )

Norman, born and raised in Louisville, Kentucky, returned there after college to begin a long and fruitful association with The Actors Theater of Louisville. They produced her fist play, <u>Getting Out</u> (1977); she wrote a series of one-act plays-- including <u>Third and Oak: The Laundromat</u>--for the theater during her 1978 NEA-funded tenure as playwright-in-residence, and their actors starred in the Broadway production of her Pulitzer-Prize-winning play, <u>'night, Mother</u> (1983). Her most recent play,

Traveller in the Dark (1984), deals with a cancer researcher who suffers a crisis of faith after being unable to save a colleague from cancer. In a recent interview Norman has claimed that each of her plays is inspired by "an emotional memory."

HAROLD PINTER (1930-   )

Pinter, the son of a Jewish tailor, was born in London and grew up in East End's working-class neighborhoods. He calimed conscientious-objector status during World War II and was fined but not imprisoned for refusing to join the armed services. Attending the Royal Academy of Dramatic Art on scholarship, Pinter went on to tour as an actor under the stage name of David Baron. His one-act play The Room aroused some interest, but his first full-length play, The Birthday Party (1958), closed in a week to bad reviews in its initial London run. It was successfully revived a year later, and The Caretaker (1960) solidified his reputation. Betrayal, about a love triangle in which each of the participants betrays the other two, was produced in 1978, and The Hothouse, though written much earlier, in 1980. Pinter is one of the most complex and difficult playwrights in post-war Britain. His plays are marked by colloquial speech and an apparent lack of "meaning" in the usual sense. Pinter has also written many film adaptations including The Servant, The Go-Between, and the screenplay of Proust's Remembrance of Things Past.

WILLIAM SHAKESPEARE (1564-1616)

Shakespeare was born of a respectable middle-class family in the town of Stratford-on-Avon, to which he retired in 1611 after a successful theatrical career in London. He became an actor in a theatrical company headed by James Burbage. The record of the roles he played indicates that he was a journeyman actor who played in support of Richard Burbage, the star of the company and the first interpreter of the great Shakespearean heroes. Although exact dates are uncertain, Shakespeare began to write plays for the company around 1590, and by 1592 he was successful enough to merit the printed scorn of the poet, playwright, and wit Robert Greene. He became a shareholder in the company and profited personally from the success which led the company to the construction of its famous theater, the Globe, in 1599 and to the privilege of bearing the name The

King's Men in 1603. During his lifetime plays were not regarded as real "literary" efforts, and dramatists were not interested in having them printed. Indeed, since there was no system of copyright, theatrical managers and playwrights preferred that they remain safely in manuscript. Most of Shakespeare's work therefore survives in pirated versions printed during his lifetime and in the monumental collection of his plays edited by his former colleagues in 1623, the First Folio. Hamlet (or The Tragedy of Hamlet, Prince of Denmark) appears to have been written about 1600 during a period of prosperity and maturity for the company and for Shakespeare.

SOPHOCLES (ca. 496-406 B.C.)

Sophocles was the son of a well-to-do Athenian armorer. He was a man of unusual talents which were recognized early and honored by his fellow citizens. After some experience as an actor, he entered the annual dramatic competition associated with the feast of Dionysus and won first prize, defeating his distinguished predecessor, Aeschylus. He wrote some 120 tragedies and won the first prize more often than any of his rivals. He was, according to Aristotle, the first to use three actors instead of two.

OSCAR WILDE (1854-1900)

Wilde was born in Dublin, the son of a prominent surgeon, and attended the university there and at Oxford. He was early associated with the so-called aesthetic movement, known as much for his eccentric behavior as for the lush decadence of his writing. He wrote in many forms, fairy tales, autobiography, poetry, a novel, essays. He is best-known now, however, as a writer of plays, and The Importance of Being Earnest (1895) is the best of his dramatic work. Wilde's later years were clouded by his conviction and subsequent imprisonment for homosexuality. After his release he went to France, where he lived under an assumed name until his death.